Preface

Welcome to the world of English Olympiad MCQ With Solutions Class 6. We're thrilled to have you start this journey, which will open doors to new experiences, ideas, and connections. English is more than just a subject in school—it's a valuable skill that can enhance every part of your life, from making friends to exploring cultures, watching movies, and even navigating the internet. With English, you gain a tool to connect with people worldwide, express your thoughts clearly, and explore the richness of global literature, media, and knowledge.

This book is designed to make learning English enjoyable, practical, and comprehensive. Whether you're new to the language or have some experience, each chapter will guide you in mastering vocabulary, grammar, speaking, reading, writing, and listening skills. Through engaging stories, relatable characters, and fun activities, this book helps you see English in action and understand its power as a language of communication, creativity, and expression.

We follow the principles of the **National Education Policy (NEP) 2020**, which emphasises holistic, competency-based, and enjoyable learning. The NEP encourages practical skills, critical thinking, and meaningful engagement, and this book is designed to meet these goals. With every lesson, you'll build valuable competencies in academics and real-world situations. We've included activities and scenarios that bring English to life, from simple conversations to meaningful self-expression.

Additionally, we have integrated lessons that connect with the **Sustainable Development Goals (SDGs)**, such as Quality Education, Gender Equality, Climate Action, and Peace and Justice. These goals encourage students to understand global challenges and work toward a better world. By learning English in this international context, you'll gain language skills and become more aware of how to contribute positively to the world.

As you read the book, remember that language learning is a gradual journey. Practice regularly, celebrate your progress, and enjoy the process. With each chapter, you'll discover the joy of expressing yourself, learning about new topics, and connecting with the world through English. We hope this book becomes a helpful companion in your journey. Happy learning!

Table of Contents

Chapter 1 - Who Did Patrick's Homework?

Q1 What did Patrick dislike doing?
a. Homework
b. Playing sports
c. Reading books
d. Cooking
Answer a. Homework

Q2 Who is the main character in the story "Who Did Patrick's Homework?"
a. Patrick
b. A teacher
c. A dog
d. A cat
Answer a. Patrick

Q3 Who did Patrick find in his room one day?
a. A little elf
b. His friend
c. A magician
d. A teacher
Answer a. A little elf

Q4 What did the elf agree to do for Patrick?
a. Help him with his homework
b. Clean his room
c. Give him toys
d. Sing for him
Answer a. Help him with his homework

Q5 The elf had trouble understanding
a. Basic subjects like math and English
b. Magic spells
c. Cooking recipes
d. Writing stories
Answer a. Basic subjects like math and English

Q6 What was the elf's condition for helping Patrick?
a. Patrick had to provide him with everything he needed
b. Patrick had to finish all his homework
c. Patrick had to give him a gift
d. Patrick had to sing
Answer a. Patrick had to provide him with everything he needed

Q7 How did Patrick feel about his homework after the elf helped him?
a. He became responsible and hardworking
b. He continued disliking it
c. He ignored it

d. He felt annoyed
Answer a. He became responsible and hardworking

Q8 What did Patrick do to help the elf complete his homework?
a. Searched for books and explanations
b. Slept
c. Played outside
d. Watched TV
Answer a. Searched for books and explanations

Q9 Why did the elf need Patrick's help?
a. He did not understand school subjects
b. He was lazy
c. He lost his magic powers
d. He wanted to make friends
Answer a. He did not understand school subjects

Q10 What change occurred in Patrick by the end of the story?
a. He became a responsible student
b. He remained lazy
c. He disliked the elf
d. He stopped going to school
Answer a. He became a responsible student

Q11 What kind of person was Patrick before the elf arrived?
a. Lazy and irresponsible
b. Studious and hardworking
c. Friendly
d. Polite
Answer a. Lazy and irresponsible

Q12 How long did the elf stay to help Patrick?
a. For 35 days
b. For 10 days
c. For a week
d. For a month
Answer a. For 35 days

Q13 Why did Patrick think his homework was getting done easily?
a. He had the help of the elf
b. He liked doing homework
c. He was good at it
d. His friend helped him
Answer a. He had the help of the elf

Q14 By the end of the story, Patrick realized that
a. Doing his own homework made him more responsible
b. Homework was easy
c. The elf would always help him

d. He didn't need to study
Answer a. Doing his own homework made him more responsible

Q15 The story "Who Did Patrick's Homework?" teaches us about
a. Responsibility and hard work
b. Magic and spells
c. Playing all the time
d. Ignoring homework
Answer a. Responsibility and hard work

Q16 Patrick's behavior improved because
a. He became involved in his studies
b. He got a new teacher
c. He stopped studying
d. He went on vacation
Answer a. He became involved in his studies

Q17 The elf struggled with subjects like
a. Math and history
b. Music
c. Dance
d. Sports
Answer a. Math and history

Q18 How did Patrick help himself while helping the elf?
a. He learned about various subjects
b. He went to play
c. He ignored the elf
d. He slept
Answer a. He learned about various subjects

Q19 What did the elf secretly teach Patrick?
a. To study independently
b. To play games
c. To avoid work
d. To ignore rules
Answer a. To study independently

Q20 Patrick's attitude towards homework changed because
a. He realized the value of learning
b. He disliked the elf
c. He made a new friend
d. He didn't have any work left
Answer a. He realized the value of learning

Chapter 2 - A House, A Home

Q1 What is a house made of, according to the poem?
a. Bricks and cement
b. Dreams
c. Love and care
d. Nature
Answer a. Bricks and cement

Q2 Which of the following is not mentioned as part of a house in the poem?
a. Bricks
b. Nails
c. Love
d. Roof
Answer c. Love

Q3 A home, according to the poem, is a place where
a. Family lives together with love and care
b. People stay alone
c. Strangers gather
d. Friends meet sometimes
Answer a. Family lives together with love and care

Q4 The poet suggests that a house and a home are
a. Different in essence
b. The same thing
c. Both made of wood
d. Temporary places
Answer a. Different in essence

Q5 What makes a home special compared to a house?
a. Love, kindness, and warmth
b. Expensive decorations
c. Colorful walls
d. New furniture
Answer a. Love, kindness, and warmth

Q6 Which of the following is true about a house in the poem?
a. It is made of lifeless materials
b. It has no family members
c. It can talk
d. It's a living place
Answer a. It is made of lifeless materials

Q7 What does a family add to a house to make it a home?
a. Love and care
b. Furniture
c. Extra rooms
d. New floors
Answer a. Love and care

Q8 A house turns into a home when
a. It is filled with the warmth of family members
b. It is painted beautifully
c. It has lots of rooms
d. It is built with expensive materials
Answer a. It is filled with the warmth of family members

Q9 According to the poem, a house is more about
a. Structure and materials
b. Love and laughter
c. Friends and guests
d. Nature and beauty
Answer a. Structure and materials

Q10 Which quality makes a place a home rather than a house?
a. Mutual understanding among family members
b. Expensive walls
c. Design and color
d. Size and height
Answer a. Mutual understanding among family members

Q11 The poem suggests that a house is
a. A structure without emotions
b. A place of joy
c. Always small
d. Made only for gatherings
Answer a. A structure without emotions

Q12 A home is where people
a. Feel a sense of belonging and togetherness
b. Always keep quiet
c. Live without interaction
d. Never talk to each other
Answer a. Feel a sense of belonging and togetherness

Q13 Which of these words is associated with a home in the poem?
a. Kindness
b. Cement
c. Furniture
d. Doors
Answer a. Kindness

Q14 The poem "A House, A Home" highlights the importance of
a. Family and relationships
b. Keeping a big house
c. Building structures
d. Decorating with flowers
Answer a. Family and relationships

Q15 How does the poem differentiate between a house and a home?
a. A house is a structure; a home is a place filled with emotions
b. A home is bigger than a house
c. A house is cheap
d. A home is just a design
Answer a. A house is a structure; a home is a place filled with emotions

Q16 The poet's view of a home is that it is a place filled with
a. Love and understanding
b. Concrete and bricks
c. Only basic items
d. Quietness
Answer a. Love and understanding

Q17 According to the poet, a house is made of
a. Walls, bricks, and plaster
b. Happiness
c. Friends
d. Peace
Answer a. Walls, bricks, and plaster

Q18 Which of these elements would not be found in a home, according to the poem?
a. Silence and separation
b. Kindness
c. Warmth
d. Family support
Answer a. Silence and separation

Q19 The main message of the poem "A House, A Home" is that
a. A home is about relationships and love, not materials
b. A house is always better
c. People should stay alone
d. Bigger homes are happier
Answer a. A home is about relationships and love, not materials

Q20 A home is special because it is filled with
a. People who care for one another
b. Only expensive items
c. Just four walls
d. Books and gadgets
Answer a. People who care for one another

Chapter 3 - How the Dog Found Himself a New Master!

Q1 The story "How the Dog Found Himself a New Master!" is about
a. A dog looking for a strong master
b. A dog making friends with a cat
c. A dog that lives alone
d. A dog building a house
Answer a. A dog looking for a strong master

Q2 Why did the dog leave his original way of life?
a. He was tired of being afraid and living alone
b. He wanted to travel
c. He was bored
d. He wanted to join a circus
Answer a. He was tired of being afraid and living alone

Q3 The first master the dog chose was
a. A wolf
b. A lion
c. A human
d. A bear
Answer a. A wolf

Q4 Why did the dog leave the wolf as a master?
a. The wolf was afraid of the bear
b. The wolf was too slow
c. The wolf didn't like the dog
d. The wolf went away
Answer a. The wolf was afraid of the bear

Q5 After leaving the wolf, the dog chose the
a. Bear as his master
b. Tiger as his master
c. Human as his master
d. Lion as his master
Answer a. Bear as his master

Q6 The dog left the bear because
a. The bear was afraid of the lion
b. The bear was not strong
c. The bear was too lazy
d. The bear was angry
Answer a. The bear was afraid of the lion

Q7 Which animal did the dog choose after the bear?
a. The lion
b. The elephant
c. The rabbit
d. The cat
Answer a. The lion

Q8 Why did the dog leave the lion as a master?
a. The lion was afraid of humans
b. The lion was too old
c. The lion was lazy
d. The lion wanted to eat the dog
Answer a. The lion was afraid of humans

Q9 Who did the dog finally choose as his master?
a. Humans
b. Lions
c. Bears
d. Wolves
Answer a. Humans

Q10 The story teaches that the dog wanted a master who was
a. Stronger than all others
b. Friendly with everyone
c. Very quiet
d. Very old
Answer a. Stronger than all others

Q11 The dog became the loyal friend of humans because
a. He found humans were the strongest
b. He liked human food
c. Humans never slept
d. He had no choice
Answer a. He found humans were the strongest

Q12 How does the dog feel about his final choice of a master?
a. Happy and loyal
b. Sad
c. Disappointed
d. Uncertain
Answer a. Happy and loyal

Q13 According to the story, the dog wanted to find a master who
a. Would protect him from danger
b. Would let him live alone
c. Was afraid of others
d. Was very young
Answer a. Would protect him from danger

Q14 The story "How the Dog Found Himself a New Master!" is mainly about
a. Loyalty and finding the best protector
b. Learning to be independent
c. Finding a new home
d. Chasing other animals
Answer a. Loyalty and finding the best protector

Q15 When the dog chose a new master each time, it was because
a. He was seeking strength and safety
b. He wanted more food
c. He wanted to be alone
d. He didn't like anyone
Answer a. He was seeking strength and safety

Q16 The bear was afraid of
a. The lion
b. The dog
c. Humans
d. Birds
Answer a. The lion

Q17 The lion was afraid of
a. Humans
b. Wolves
c. Trees
d. Bears
Answer a. Humans

Q18 The story explains why dogs are loyal to
a. Humans
b. Wolves
c. Lions
d. Bears
Answer a. Humans

Q19 The dog's journey to find a master teaches us about
a. Finding strength and security
b. Making friends with everyone
c. Living in the forest
d. Becoming very strong
Answer a. Finding strength and security

Q20 The main lesson from the story is that
a. Dogs are loyal to humans because they are strong and protective
b. Wolves are the best friends of dogs
c. Bears are very friendly
d. Lions are the strongest
Answer a. Dogs are loyal to humans because they are strong and protective

Chapter 4 - The Kite

Q1 What is the main subject of the poem "The Kite"?
a. A colourful kite flying in the sky
b. A bird in the trees
c. A mountain
d. A river
Answer a. A colourful kite flying in the sky

Q2 In the poem, the kite looks bright and beautiful when it
a. Rises high in the sky
b. Falls down
c. Lies on the ground
d. Gets tangled in a tree
Answer a. Rises high in the sky

Q3 The kite moves in the sky with
a. Grace and swiftness
b. Slow movements
c. Difficulty
d. Confusion
Answer a. Grace and swiftness.

Q4 What happens to the kite when the wind stops blowing?
a. It falls down
b. It flies higher
c. It spins in circles
d. It moves faster
Answer a. It falls.

Q5 In the poem, what does the kite do when it dips?
a. It moves downwards
b. It goes up
c. It spins around
d. It stays still
Answer a. It moves downwards.

Q6 How does the poet describe the movement of the kite?
a. It moves with a zigzag motion
b. It falls flat
c. It stays in one place
d. It is ultimately still
Answer a. It moves with a zigzag motion

Q7 When the kite flies high, it seems to be
a. Bright and full of colours
b. Dull and lifeless
c. Moving slowly
d. Stuck in one place
Answer a. Bright and full of colors

Q8 The poet compares the kite's movement to
a. A dancer's movement in the air
b. A bird in a cage
c. A car on the road
d. A tree in the wind
Answer a. A dancer's movement in the air

Q9 According to the poet, when the wind blows, the kite
a. Dips and dives
b. Falls down
c. Spins wildly
d. Stays still
Answer a. Dips and dives.

Q10 How does the kite appear when it is newly made?
a. Fresh and bright
b. Dull and plain
c. Old and worn
d. Light and fragile
Answer a. Fresh and bright.

Q11 When the kite gets caught, it
a. Flaps on the string
b. Flies even higher
c. Spins in circles
d. Falls on the ground
Answer a. Flaps on the string.

Q12 The poem describes the kite as
a. Majestic and beautiful in the sky
b. Heavy and grounded
c. Plain and simple
d. Fragile
Answer a. Majestic and beautiful in the sky

Q13 The kite looks lifeless when
a. It gets torn
b. It flies high
c. It dips down
d. The wind blows
Answer a. It gets torn.

Q14 The poem uses imagery to make readers
a. Visualize the kite's beauty and movement
b. Think of a bird
c. Picture a mountain
d. Imagine a rainbow
Answer a. Visualize the kite's beauty and movement

Q15 What does the kite look like when it's torn?
a. A piece of paper fluttering
b. A strong rope
c. A tree branch
d. A thick cloud
Answer a. A piece of paper fluttering

Q16 The kite's journey in the sky is described as
a. Both graceful and lively
b. Completely still
c. Very heavy
d. Boring
Answer a. Both are graceful and lively.

Q17 The poem captures the beauty of the kite through its
a. Movements and colours
b. Size and weight
c. Material
d. Sound
Answer a. Movements and colours.

Q18 The central theme of "The Kite" is
a. The elegance and freedom of a kite in the sky
b. The silence of nature
c. The loneliness of the forest
d. The beauty of birds
Answer a. The elegance and freedom of a kite in the sky

Q19 The kite's flight is a symbol of
a. Joy and freedom
b. Sadness
c. Anger
d. Loneliness
Answer a. Joy and freedom.

Q20 The poet describes the kite as looking best when it
a. Sails in the air with a bright hue
b. Lies on the ground
c. Is torn and tangled
d. Spins in the rain
Answer a. Sails in the air with a bright hue.

Chapter 5 - Taro's Reward

Q1 Who is the main character in the story "Taro's Reward"?
a. Taro, a young woodcutter
b. A fisherman named Taro
c. A soldier
d. A merchant
Answer a. Taro, a young woodcutter.

Q2 Taro worked very hard to
a. Take care of his parents
b. Build a house
c. Buy new clothes
d. Save money
Answer a. Take care of his parents

Q3 What did Taro wish he could provide for his father?
a. A warm cup of sake
b. A comfortable chair
c. A new sword
d. A large meal
Answer a. A warm cup of sake

Q4 Why did Taro's father want sake?
a. He was feeling cold
b. He was celebrating
c. He was tired
d. He was working
Answer a. He was feeling cold.

Q5 What did Taro find flowing from the waterfall?
a. Sweet sake instead of water
b. Gold coins
c. Fruits
d. Honey
Answer a. Sweet sake instead of water

Q6 The waterfall that Taro discovered was
a. Magical and produced sake
b. A usual waterfall
c. In the middle of a desert
d. Surrounded by animals
Answer a. Magical and produced sake.

Q7 When other villagers heard about the waterfall, they
a. Rushed to see it
b. Ignored it
c. Planted trees around it
d. Closed it off
Answer a. Rushed to see it.

Q8 What did the villagers find when they reached the waterfall?
a. Only plain water
b. More sake
c. Gold coins
d. Sweets
Answer a. Only plain water.

Q9 Why did the Emperor reward Taro?
a. For his love and care for his parents
b. To save the villagers
c. For building a house
d. For making a discovery
Answer a. For his love and care for his parents

Q10 Taro was rewarded because he was
a. Hardworking and kind-hearted
b. Strong
c. A famous person
d. Very quiet
Answer a. Hardworking and kind-hearted.

Q11 The story "Taro's Reward" teaches us about
a. Respecting and caring for parents
b. Staying away from people
c. Ignoring family
d. Only working for oneself
Answer a. Respecting and caring for parents

Q12 How did Taro's hard work pay off?
a. He found a magical waterfall that provided sake
b. He bought a new house
c. He made new friends
d. He earned a lot of money
Answer a. He found a magical waterfall that provided sake

Q13 The villagers were disappointed when they
a. Found only water at the waterfall
b. Found the waterfall dry
c. Couldn't reach the waterfall
d. Saw Taro with sake
Answer a. Found only water at the waterfall

Q14 The Emperor rewarded Taro to
a. Set an example of respect and kindness
b. Make him a prince
c. Make him leave the village
d. Give him wealth
Answer a. Set an example of respect and kindness

Q15 Taro's story is an example of
a. Love and dedication towards family
b. Traveling around the world
c. Hunting and gathering
d. Being a warrior
Answer a. Love and dedication towards family

Q16 Taro worked harder than others because
a. He wanted to help his family
b. He wanted to buy expensive clothes
c. He was greedy
d. He disliked others
Answer a. He wanted to help his family

Q17 The magical waterfall stopped giving sake because
a. The villagers came with greedy intentions
b. Taro closed it
c. It dried up
d. It was a seasonal spring
Answer a. The villagers came with greedy intentions

Q18 The story teaches that hard work and good intentions lead to
a. Unexpected rewards
b. Punishment
c. Laziness
d. Disappointments
Answer a. Unexpected rewards.

Q19 How did Taro feel when he found the sake?
a. Happy and grateful
b. Angry
c. Scared
d. Sad
Answer a. Happy and grateful.

Q20 The Emperor's message to the people was to
a. Follow Taro's example of respect for elders
b. Ignore others
c. Find new waterfalls
d. Seek wealth
Answer a. Follow Taro's example of respect for elders.

Chapter 6 - The Quarrel

Q1 The poem "The Quarrel" is about
a. A fight between siblings
b. A war
c. A game
d. A celebration
Answer a. A fight between siblings.

Q2 Who are the two characters in the poem?
a. A brother and a sister
b. Two friends
c. Two teachers
d. Two animals
Answer a. A brother and a sister

Q3 How does the quarrel begin?
a. Over a slight misunderstanding
b. With a loud argument
c. By stealing a toy
d. With a long conversation
Answer a. Over a slight misunderstanding.

Q4 In the poem, the quarrel is described as
a. Starting for no reason
b. A planned argument
c. A big event
d. About serious issues
Answer a. Starting for no reason.

Q5 Who feels that they are right in the quarrel?
a. Both the brother and the sister
b. Only the sister
c. Only the brother
d. A friend
Answer a. Both the brother and the sister

Q6 What changes their attitude towards each other?
a. They realise that the fight is unnecessary
b. Their parents arrive
c. Their friends help
d. They leave each other alone
Answer a. They realise that the fight is unnecessary

Q7 Who apologises first in the poem?
a. The brother
b. The sister
c. Their friend
d. Their teacher
Answer a. The brother

Q8 The brother says, "I was wrong" to
a. Make peace with his sister
b. Win the argument
c. Ignore his sister
d. Leave the house
Answer a. Make peace with his sister

Q9 The poem shows that quarrels between siblings are
a. Common but quickly resolved
b. Rare and serious
c. Never-ending
d. Always violent
Answer a. Common but quickly resolved.

Q10 What feeling do the siblings have after making up?
a. Happiness and relief
b. Anger
c. Sadness
d. Fear
Answer a. Happiness and relief.

Q11 The poem suggests that quarrels often start
a. Without any big reason
b. With a severe issue
c. over money
d. Because of parents
Answer a. Without any significant reason.

Q12 What lesson can we learn from the poem?
a. Fights don't solve problems; understanding does
b. Fighting is necessary
c. Being angry is important
d. Winning is all that matters
Answer a. Fights don't solve problems; understanding does

Q13 How does the poet describe the end of the quarrel?
a. With a happy tone
b. With a sad tone
c. With anger
d. With confusion
Answer a. With a happy tone.

Q14 In the poem, the quarrel is resolved by
a. Talking and apologising
b. Ignoring each other
c. Fighting more
d. Asking for help
Answer a. Talking and apologising.

Q15 The quarrel made the siblings feel
a. Unhappy but later relieved
b. Very excited
c. Very confused
d. Joyful at first
Answer a. Unhappy but later relieved.

Q16 Quarrels can be solved with
a. Apologies and understanding
b. More arguments
c. Silence
d. Anger
Answer a. Apologies and understanding.

Q17 The poem's theme is
a. The importance of harmony in relationships
b. The value of winning fights
c. Ignoring family members
d. Spending time alone
Answer a. The importance of harmony in relationships

Q18 The siblings' quarrel was about
a. A small and silly matter
b. A big issue
c. Money
d. Food
Answer a. A small and silly matter

Q19 The brother's willingness to apologise shows
a. Maturity and kindness
b. Anger
c. Selfishness
d. Pride
Answer a. Maturity and kindness.

Q20 The poem teaches us that misunderstandings
a. Can be resolved with kindness and communication
b. Should be ignored
c. Must continue
d. Are always serious
Answer a. Can be resolved with kindness and communication.

Chapter 7 - An Indian – American Woman in Space: Kalpana Chawla

Q1 Who is the main subject of the story "An Indian – American Woman in Space"?
a. Kalpana Chawla
b. Rakesh Sharma
c. Sunita Williams
d. Neil Armstrong
Answer a. Kalpana Chawla.

Q2 Kalpana Chawla was the first woman of Indian origin to
a. Travel to space
b. Climb Mount Everest
c. Become a scientist
d. Win a Nobel Prize
Answer a. Travel to space.

Q3 Kalpana Chawla's birthplace was
a. Karnal, Haryana
b. Delhi
c. Mumbai
d. Kolkata
Answer a. Karnal, Haryana.

Q4 Kalpana Chawla pursued her higher education in
a. The United States
b. Canada
c. Japan
d. France
Answer a. The United States

Q5 Kalpana studied to become
a. An astronaut and an engineer
b. A doctor
c. A pilot
d. A teacher
Answer a. An astronaut and an engineer

Q6 Kalpana's first mission to space was aboard the
a. Space Shuttle Columbia
b. Space Shuttle Challenger
c. Space Shuttle Atlantis
d. Space Shuttle Endeavour
Answer a. Space Shuttle Columbia.

Q7 Kalpana Chawla was known for her.
a. Bravery and commitment to science
b. Singing
c. Writing skills
d. Acting
Answer a. Bravery and commitment to science.

Q8 In which year did Kalpana's first space mission take place?
a. 1997
b. 2000
c. 1990
d. 1985
Answer a. 1997

Q9 Kalpana's final space mission tragically ended because
a. The Space Shuttle Columbia broke apart during re-entry
b. She decided to stay in space
c. She returned safely but was injured
d. A meteor hit the shuttle
Answer a. The Space Shuttle Columbia broke apart during re-entry

Q10 How did Kalpana's achievements impact Indian girls and women?
a. She became an inspiration for aspiring astronauts
b. It led them to avoid science
c. It had no effect
d. It made them prefer other jobs
Answer a. She became an inspiration for aspiring astronauts

Q11 The story of Kalpana Chawla is one of
a. Courage and ambition
b. Wealth and fame
c. Fear and isolation
d. Silence
Answer a. Courage and ambition.

Q12 Kalpana's dedication to her field shows that with determination, one can
a. Overcome barriers and achieve their dreams
b. Only work in their hometown
c. Avoid hard work
d. Ignore their studies
Answer a. Overcome barriers and achieve their dreams

Q13 The tragic end of Kalpana's mission reminds us about
a. The risks involved in space exploration
b. The need to avoid space travel
c. The fear of heights
d. The end of science
Answer a. The risks involved in space exploration

Q14 Kalpana was a citizen of which country during her space missions?
a. The United States
b. India
c. Canada
d. Russia
Answer a. The United States

Q15 Kalpana's contribution to space science is remembered for her
a. Courage, skill, and inspiration to others
b. Love for money
c. Political achievements
d. Personal wealth
Answer a. Courage, skill, and inspiration to others

Q16 Kalpana Chawla's life story motivates people to
a. Dream big and work hard
b. Avoid science
c. Focus only on wealth
d. Stay in their birthplace
Answer a. Dream big and work hard

Q17 How did Kalpana's parents support her dream?
a. They encouraged her to study whatever she liked
b. They told her to stay home
c. They forced her to work in a different field
d. They discouraged her from science
Answer a. They encouraged her to study whatever she liked

Q18 Kalpana Chawla's life exemplifies
a. Breaking boundaries and achieving extraordinary
b. Avoiding travel
c. Following traditions only
d. Ignoring education
Answer a. Breaking boundaries and achieving the extraordinary

Q19 Kalpana was fascinated by aeroplanes as
a. A child
b. An adult
c. A teacher
d. A friend
Answer a. A child

Q20 Kalpana Chawla's story is celebrated because she
a. Showed that anyone can reach for the stars with hard work
b. Stayed away from her dreams
c. Became a dancer
d. Only followed others
Answer a. Showed that anyone can reach for the stars with hard work.

Chapter 8 - Beauty

Q1 According to the poem "Beauty," beauty can be seen in
a. Nature and simple things around us
b. Only expensive things
c. Only famous people
d. Bright colors only
Answer a. Nature and simple things around us

Q2 The poet suggests that beauty is present in
a. Good deeds and kind actions
b. Only loud sounds
c. Harsh actions
d. Large buildings
Answer a. Good deeds and kind actions

Q3 Beauty can be heard in
a. The sound of rain, birds, and flowing streams
b. Loud music
c. Shouting
d. Silence only
Answer a. The sound of rain, birds, and flowing streams

Q4 According to the poem, beauty lies in
a. Both what we see and what we hear
b. Only what we own
c. Material wealth
d. Fame
Answer a. Both what we see and what we hear

Q5 Beauty is described as something that can be
a. Found in nature and daily activities
b. Only in big cities
c. Rare and unreachable
d. Visible only in books
Answer a. Found in nature and daily activities

Q6 Beauty is in the eyes of
a. The beholder
b. Only the artist
c. Famous people
d. Celebrities
Answer a. The beholder

Q7 The poet feels that beauty is in actions that
a. Are good and positive
b. Are selfish
c. Are harmful
d. Cause sadness
Answer a. Are good and positive

Q8 What does the poet say about inner beauty?
a. It is present in good thoughts and kind hearts
b. It is invisible
c. It is only seen in rich people
d. It fades quickly
Answer a. It is present in good thoughts and kind hearts

Q9 The poem suggests that beauty is
a. Everywhere if we have eyes to see it
b. Rare and hidden
c. Only in the mountains
d. Only found in people
Answer a. Everywhere if we have eyes to see it

Q10 Beauty can be heard in the night through
a. Whispering winds and silent skies
b. Loud noises
c. Television
d. Screaming
Answer a. Whispering winds and silent skies

Q11 According to the poem, true beauty is found in
a. Thoughts and deeds that help others
b. Expensive things
c. Showy appearances
d. Fame
Answer a. Thoughts and deeds that help others

Q12 The poet encourages readers to
a. Find beauty in simple, everyday things
b. Look only for money
c. Ignore nature
d. Seek fame
Answer a. Find beauty in simple, everyday things

Q13 The poem suggests that beauty is a feeling that
a. We experience within and around us
b. Is only in cities
c. Comes from wealth
d. Can be ignored
Answer a. We experience within and around us

Q14 Beauty in actions comes from
a. Good intentions and positive outcomes
b. Money only
c. Anger
d. Arguments
Answer a. Good intentions and positive outcomes

Q15 How does the poet describe beauty at night?
a. In peaceful and quiet scenes
b. In loud music
c. In storms only
d. In television shows
Answer a. In peaceful and quiet scenes

Q16 The poem "Beauty" teaches us to appreciate
a. Both inner and outer beauty
b. Only outer appearances
c. Expensive items only
d. Noise
Answer a. Both inner and outer beauty

Q17 Beauty can be experienced in nature through
a. Gentle and soothing sounds
b. Loud music
c. Bright lights
d. Urban noise
Answer a. Gentle and soothing sounds

Q18 The poet believes that beauty is found in people who
a. Have kind and gentle thoughts
b. Are rich
c. Are famous
d. Are silent
Answer a. Have kind and gentle thoughts

Q19 Beauty lies in
a. Our perception and appreciation of life's details
b. Famous personalities only
c. Wealth only
d. Avoiding nature
Answer a. Our perception and appreciation of life's details

Q20 The poem teaches us that beauty
a. Is present all around us if we are open to it
b. Is rare
c. Exists only in objects
d. Only exists at certain times
Answer a. Is present all around us if we are open to it

Chapter 9 - A Different Kind of School

Q1 What is unique about Miss Beam's school?
a. It teaches kindness and empathy through special days
b. It has only one classroom
c. It focuses only on sports
d. It has no exams
Answer a. It teaches kindness and empathy through special days

Q2 The special days at Miss Beam's school are called
a. Blind Day, Dumb Day, and Lame Day
b. Happy Day
c. Sports Day
d. Holiday
Answer a. Blind Day, Dumb Day, and Lame Day

Q3 On "Blind Day," students experience what it's like to
a. Be blind and depend on others
b. Eat new foods
c. Read many books
d. Stay alone
Answer a. Be blind and depend on others

Q4 The main purpose of these special days is to teach students
a. Empathy and understanding for others' challenges
b. How to study better
c. How to dance
d. To avoid others
Answer a. Empathy and understanding for others' challenges

Q5 How do students help each other on special days?
a. By guiding and supporting one another
b. By ignoring each other
c. By teasing
d. By leaving school
Answer a. By guiding and supporting one another

Q6 Miss Beam's school focuses on
a. Building kindness and compassion
b. Only academics
c. Sports competitions
d. Keeping students silent
Answer a. Building kindness and compassion

Q7 On "Lame Day," students experience what it's like to
a. Be unable to walk and need assistance
b. Sing songs
c. Dance well
d. Be alone
Answer a. Be unable to walk and need assistance

Q8 The author's initial impression of the school was that it was
a. Unusual and different
b. Ordinary
c. Very strict
d. Large and noisy
Answer a. Unusual and different

Q9 Miss Beam's teaching method encourages students to
a. Develop empathy and gratitude
b. Focus only on academics
c. Ignore others
d. Be competitive
Answer a. Develop empathy and gratitude

Q10 The school's approach helps students understand
a. The difficulties faced by differently-abled people
b. The joy of being wealthy
c. How to read faster
d. How to solve puzzles
Answer a. The difficulties faced by differently-abled people

Q11 The students at Miss Beam's school learn
a. By experiencing challenges faced by others
b. By sitting quietly
c. By reading many books
d. Through only exams
Answer a. By experiencing challenges faced by others

Q12 On "Dumb Day," students experience
a. Being unable to speak
b. Reading stories
c. Painting pictures
d. Writing poems
Answer a. Being unable to speak

Q13 The atmosphere at Miss Beam's school is described as
a. Kind and helpful
b. Very strict
c. Competitive
d. Noisy
Answer a. Kind and helpful

Q14 The special days are intended to develop
a. Sensitivity and consideration towards others
b. Only reading skills
c. Math skills
d. Independence
Answer a. Sensitivity and consideration towards others

Q15 Miss Beam's school gives students a chance to
a. Experience life from another perspective
b. Travel to other cities
c. Study alone
d. Avoid studies
Answer a. Experience life from another perspective

Q16 The teacher at the school, Miss Beam, is known for her
a. Innovative approach to teaching
b. Strict rules
c. Love of sports
d. Quiet nature
Answer a. Innovative approach to teaching

Q17 The school's lessons are not just academic; they focus on
a. Building empathy and social skills
b. Only writing
c. Competition
d. Discipline
Answer a. Building empathy and social skills

Q18 The students at Miss Beam's school are encouraged to
a. Help each other and understand each other's difficulties
b. Read alone
c. Avoid challenges
d. Only talk to their friends
Answer a. Help each other and understand each other's difficulties

Q19 The lessons at the school leave a lasting impact by
a. Encouraging lifelong kindness and compassion
b. Teaching about different countries
c. Avoiding hard work
d. Ignoring other people
Answer a. Encouraging lifelong kindness and compassion

Q20 The story "A Different Kind of School" teaches us that
a. Kindness and understanding can be learned through experience
b. Reading is most important
c. Discipline is the only lesson
d. Exams measure success
Answer a. Kindness and understanding can be learned through experience

Chapter 10 - Where Do All the Teachers Go?

Q1 The poem "Where Do All the Teachers Go?" is about
a. A child's curiosity about teachers' lives outside school
b. A vacation
c. A class party
d. An exam
Answer a. A child's curiosity about teachers' lives outside school

Q2 The child in the poem wonders if teachers
a. Are like regular people at home
b. Go to school all the time
c. Never leave school
d. Live at school
Answer a. Are like regular people at home

Q3 The child imagines teachers as
a. People who do normal things like cooking and cleaning
b. Superheroes
c. Always reading books
d. Sleeping all day
Answer a. People who do normal things like cooking and cleaning

Q4 The child wants to know if teachers wear
a. Regular clothes at home
b. Uniforms at all times
c. Bright colors
d. Costumes
Answer a. Regular clothes at home

Q5 The poem reflects the child's curiosity about
a. Teachers' daily lives outside school
b. School events
c. Exams and grades
d. Famous people
Answer a. Teachers' daily lives outside school

Q6 The child imagines that teachers might also
a. Watch TV and go shopping
b. Stay at school all day
c. Sing on stage
d. Travel to other countries
Answer a. Watch TV and go shopping

Q7 In the poem, the child wonders if teachers were
a. Ever young children themselves
b. Always grown-ups
c. Never made mistakes
d. Always serious
Answer a. Ever young children themselves

Q8 The poem's tone can best be described as
a. Playful and curious
b. Sad
c. Angry
d. Serious
Answer a. Playful and curious

Q9 The child is curious if teachers ever
a. Made mistakes and had fun
b. Were always perfect
c. Never left school
d. Stayed alone
Answer a. Made mistakes and had fun

Q10 The poet makes us think about the fact that teachers are
a. Just like everyone else, with daily routines and activities
b. Only focused on studies
c. Very different
d. Always strict
Answer a. Just like everyone else, with daily routines and activities

Q11 The child's questions show a desire to
a. Know teachers beyond the classroom
b. Be in the school
c. Avoid teachers
d. Ignore studies
Answer a. Know teachers beyond the classroom

Q12 The poem explores the idea that teachers are
a. Human and relatable
b. Only teachers
c. Very strict
d. Always studying
Answer a. Human and relatable

Q13 The poem ends with the child wanting to
a. Understand the real lives of teachers
b. Stay alone
c. Avoid school
d. Become a teacher
Answer a. Understand the real lives of teachers

Q14 According to the child, teachers may do things like
a. Play games, eat sweets, and get scolded
b. Travel every day
c. Be at school always
d. Fly planes
Answer a. Play games, eat sweets, and get scolded

Q15 The poem suggests that children often see teachers as
a. Different and mysterious
b. Strict
c. Always serious
d. Not interesting
Answer a. Different and mysterious

Q16 The child's curiosity leads him to think that teachers are
a. Like everyone else with their own lives
b. Only serious
c. Always angry
d. Alone
Answer a. Like everyone else with their own lives

Q17 The poet uses the child's thoughts to show that children
a. Are curious about everything around them
b. Only like school
c. Don't want teachers
d. Are always quiet
Answer a. Are curious about everything around them

Q18 The poet emphasizes that teachers
a. Are human, with ordinary lives outside the classroom
b. Live at school
c. Don't eat at home
d. Don't go out
Answer a. Are human, with ordinary lives outside the classroom

Q19 The poem's main theme is
a. The curiosity of children about teachers' lives
b. The difficulty of exams
c. The importance of sports
d. Travel
Answer a. The curiosity of children about teachers' lives

Q20 The child's view of teachers changes as he realizes
a. They are normal people with everyday habits and routines
b. They are very wealthy
c. They never make mistakes
d. They are not human
Answer a. They are normal people with everyday habits and routines

Chapter 11 - Who I Am

Q1 The chapter "Who I Am" is about
a. Self-discovery and unique qualities in people
b. Science and nature
c. Myths and legends
d. Adventure stories
Answer a. Self-discovery and unique qualities in people

Q2 Radha enjoys
a. Climbing trees
b. Playing video games
c. Reading books
d. Cooking
Answer a. Climbing trees

Q3 When climbing a tree, Radha feels
a. Excited and free
b. Tired
c. Scared
d. Angry
Answer a. Excited and free

Q4 Nasir wants to be a
a. Farmer
b. Scientist
c. Doctor
d. Teacher
Answer a. Farmer

Q5 Nasir's dream is to grow
a. Cotton
b. Wheat
c. Fruits
d. Flowers
Answer a. Cotton

Q6 Rohit loves traveling and wants to visit
a. Different countries
b. Just his village
c. Only his city
d. The mountains
Answer a. Different countries

Q7 Rohit feels fascinated by
a. New places and cultures
b. Staying indoors
c. Watching movies
d. Learning to cook
Answer a. New places and cultures

Q8 Dolma wishes to become a
a. Prime Minister
b. Scientist
c. Doctor
d. Teacher
Answer a. Prime Minister

Q9 Dolma's ambition shows her desire to
a. Help people and improve society
b. Travel to other countries
c. Avoid responsibility
d. Be quiet
Answer a. Help people and improve society

Q10 The chapter highlights that every person has
a. Unique dreams and ambitions
b. The same goals
c. No interest in anything
d. Identical preferences
Answer a. Unique dreams and ambitions

Q11 Peter enjoys spending time with
a. Friends and family
b. Strangers
c. Animals only
d. His teacher
Answer a. Friends and family

Q12 Radha's skill in climbing trees shows her love for
a. Nature and adventure
b. Staying at home
c. Studying
d. Avoiding challenges
Answer a. Nature and adventure

Q13 Nasir's interest in farming is mainly to
a. Understand and improve agricultural methods
b. Get rich
c. Become famous
d. Avoid hard work
Answer a. Understand and improve agricultural methods

Q14 Rohit's love for travel shows his curiosity about
a. Cultures and lifestyles across the world
b. Just one place
c. Old books
d. Technology
Answer a. Cultures and lifestyles across the world

Q15 Dolma's ambition shows her qualities of
a. Leadership and compassion
b. Silence
c. Wealth
d. Shyness
Answer a. Leadership and compassion

Q16 The main theme of "Who I Am" is
a. Celebrating individual differences and ambitions
b. Following the same path
c. Avoiding dreams
d. Sticking to one skill
Answer a. Celebrating individual differences and ambitions

Q17 Each character in the chapter has a unique
a. Dream or interest
b. Schedule
c. House
d. Uniform
Answer a. Dream or interest

Q18 The chapter encourages readers to
a. Embrace their unique qualities and dreams
b. Ignore their interests
c. Follow what others do
d. Stay indoors
Answer a. Embrace their unique qualities and dreams

Q19 Dolma's ambition to be a Prime Minister shows her
a. Desire to serve and lead
b. Desire to travel
c. Interest in reading
d. Focus on sports
Answer a. Desire to serve and lead

Q20 Peter's enjoyment in spending time with people shows his
a. Social nature and love for family
b. Dislike for friends
c. Interest in sports
d. Love for silence
Answer a. Social nature and love for family

Chapter 12 - The Wonderful Words

Q1 The poem "The Wonderful Words" is about
a. The power and beauty of language
b. Nature
c. Playing games
d. A visit to a new place
Answer a. The power and beauty of language

Q2 The poet encourages readers to express their ideas
a. Using beautiful and meaningful words
b. By keeping quiet
c. Only through drawing
d. By shouting
Answer a. Using beautiful and meaningful words

Q3 According to the poet, words are like
a. Magical tools to express thoughts
b. Sharp objects
c. Heavy weights
d. Difficult puzzles
Answer a. Magical tools to express thoughts

Q4 The poet believes that each person's thoughts are
a. Unique and valuable
b. Exactly the same
c. Unnecessary
d. Easy to ignore
Answer a. Unique and valuable

Q5 The poet encourages readers to
a. Find the right words to express themselves
b. Stay silent
c. Ignore language
d. Avoid creativity
Answer a. Find the right words to express themselves

Q6 According to the poem, expressing one's ideas brings
a. Joy and clarity
b. Anger
c. Confusion
d. Fear
Answer a. Joy and clarity

Q7 The poem suggests that language can be
a. A way to share and understand others
b. Only for reading books
c. A confusing subject
d. Easy to ignore
Answer a. A way to share and understand others

Q8 The poet encourages readers to
a. Share their thoughts confidently
b. Avoid speaking
c. Speak in a low tone
d. Use few words
Answer a. Share their thoughts confidently

Q9 The poem celebrates language as
a. A bridge for communication and creativity
b. A hard task
c. A difficult subject
d. A quiet hobby
Answer a. A bridge for communication and creativity

Q10 The poet compares words to
a. Magic that brings thoughts to life
b. Heavy stones
c. Colors
d. Big clouds
Answer a. Magic that brings thoughts to life

Q11 The message of the poem is to
a. Embrace and use language to communicate ideas
b. Speak only when needed
c. Remain silent
d. Avoid expressing ideas
Answer a. Embrace and use language to communicate ideas

Q12 According to the poet, words help us
a. Share and connect with others
b. Stay hidden
c. Compete with friends
d. Make friends only
Answer a. Share and connect with others

Q13 The poet says that thoughts
a. Need words to be understood
b. Are heavy
c. Should be hidden
d. Are confusing
Answer a. Need words to be understood

Q14 The "wonderful words" allow people to
a. Bring their ideas into the world
b. Hide their feelings
c. Disagree with others
d. Stay quiet
Answer a. Bring their ideas into the world

Q15 The poet suggests that language is
a. A precious gift for everyone
b. A burden
c. Only for students
d. Hard to learn
Answer a. A precious gift for everyone

Q16 The main theme of "The Wonderful Words" is
a. The beauty and importance of expression through words
b. Avoiding speech
c. Keeping secrets
d. Playing games
Answer a. The beauty and importance of expression through words

Q17 According to the poem, words can make us
a. Share the beauty of our thoughts
b. Feel alone
c. Very tired
d. Only observe
Answer a. Share the beauty of our thoughts

Q18 The poem encourages readers to
a. Use language creatively and meaningfully
b. Avoid long sentences
c. Keep thoughts hidden
d. Speak less
Answer a. Use language creatively and meaningfully

Q19 Thoughts become meaningful when
a. We use words to express them
b. We keep them secret
c. We avoid talking
d. We write them in a diary
Answer a. We use words to express them

Q20 The poet suggests that expressing thoughts brings
a. Happiness and connection with others
b. Silence
c. Fear
d. Anger
Answer a. Happiness and connection with others

Chapter 13 - Fair Play

Q1 The story "Fair Play" is about
a. Friendship and justice
b. A sports competition
c. Building a house
d. Going on a trip
Answer a. Friendship and justice

Q2 The main characters in the story are
a. Jumman and Algu
b. Ramu and Bina
c. Ravi and Rohan
d. Surya and Ram
Answer a. Jumman and Algu

Q3 Jumman and Algu were
a. Close friends
b. Strangers
c. Brothers
d. Neighbors who disliked each other
Answer a. Close friends

Q4 Jumman's aunt transferred her property to him on the condition that
a. He would take care of her
b. She would work for him
c. She would live somewhere else
d. She would give him money
Answer a. He would take care of her

Q5 Jumman's behavior towards his aunt changed when
a. He started treating her badly after gaining the property
b. She stopped giving him money
c. She left the village
d. She moved to another house
Answer a. He started treating her badly after gaining the property

Q6 The aunt decided to take her complaint to the village panchayat because
a. Jumman was unfair to her
b. She wanted to avoid him
c. She disliked the village
d. She was planning to move
Answer a. Jumman was unfair to her

Q7 Who was chosen as the head of the panchayat to decide the case?
a. Algu
b. Ramu
c. Ravi
d. Surya
Answer a. Algu

Q8 Algu was put in a difficult position because
a. He had to give a fair decision against his friend
b. He wanted to leave the village
c. He disliked the aunt
d. He was very busy
Answer a. He had to give a fair decision against his friend

Q9 What decision did Algu make regarding Jumman's treatment of his aunt?
a. He ruled in favor of the aunt
b. He ruled in favor of Jumman
c. He postponed the decision
d. He ignored the case
Answer a. He ruled in favor of the aunt

Q10 Jumman felt betrayed by Algu because
a. Algu had supported his aunt's case
b. Algu ignored him
c. Algu moved to another town
d. Algu borrowed money from him
Answer a. Algu had supported his aunt's case

Q11 Later, Algu faced a similar situation where he needed the panchayat's help because
a. His bullock died, and he wasn't paid fairly
b. He lost his house
c. He wanted to leave the village
d. He had an argument with his family
Answer a. His bullock died, and he wasn't paid fairly

Q12 Who was chosen as the head of the panchayat when Algu's case was brought?
a. Jumman
b. Ramu
c. The aunt
d. Surya
Answer a. Jumman

Q13 Jumman's decision in Algu's case was
a. Fair and unbiased
b. Full of anger
c. Delayed for days
d. Ignored
Answer a. Fair and unbiased

Q14 In the end, Jumman and Algu
a. Forgave each other and became friends again
b. Left the village
c. Fought each other
d. Stopped talking
Answer a. Forgave each other and became friends again

Q15 The story "Fair Play" teaches the value of
a. Justice and honesty in friendships
b. Ignoring friends
c. Avoiding responsibility
d. Traveling the world
Answer a. Justice and honesty in friendships

Q16 The story shows that true friends are those who
a. Can act fairly, even against each other
b. Ignore each other's mistakes
c. Always agree with each other
d. Never argue
Answer a. Can act fairly, even against each other

Q17 Algu's fairness in the panchayat shows his
a. Integrity and moral values
b. Dislike for Jumman
c. Love for money
d. Fear of the village
Answer a. Integrity and moral values

Q18 Jumman's decision in Algu's case demonstrates
a. Growth and understanding of justice
b. Revenge
c. Anger
d. Competition
Answer a. Growth and understanding of justice

Q19 The panchayat plays a central role in the story as
a. A place for justice and fair decisions
b. A competition ground
c. A market
d. A school
Answer a. A place for justice and fair decisions

Q20 The story "Fair Play" encourages readers to
a. Act justly and uphold fairness, even when it's difficult
b. Avoid friendships
c. Ignore justice
d. Keep secrets
Answer a. Act justly and uphold fairness, even when it's difficult

Chapter 14 - A Game of Chance

Q1 The story "A Game of Chance" is about
a. A boy's experience at a fair and the lesson he learns about gambling
b. A game of cricket
c. A cooking competition
d. A visit to the zoo
Answer a. A boy's experience at a fair and the lesson he learns about gambling

Q2 Rasheed goes to the fair with
a. His uncle and a servant
b. His mother
c. His teacher
d. His sister
Answer a. His uncle and a servant

Q3 Rasheed is attracted to a game where he
a. Can win prizes by guessing numbers
b. Plays cricket
c. Buys sweets
d. Takes photos
Answer a. Can win prizes by guessing numbers

Q4 The shopkeeper convinces Rasheed that he
a. Can easily win prizes by playing
b. Should buy food
c. Will lose money
d. Should avoid the game
Answer a. Can easily win prizes by playing

Q5 Rasheed continues to play the game despite losing because
a. He believes he can win back his money
b. He is afraid to leave
c. His uncle tells him to
d. He enjoys losing
Answer a. He believes he can win back his money

Q6 What is the outcome of Rasheed's repeated attempts to win?
a. He loses all his money
b. He wins a big prize
c. He goes home early
d. He avoids the fair
Answer a. He loses all his money

Q7 Rasheed feels disappointed and realizes that the game was
a. A trick to make him lose money
b. Fun
c. Easy to win
d. Fair
Answer a. A trick to make him lose money

Q8 Rasheed's uncle teaches him that games of chance are often
a. Deceptive and designed to cheat people
b. Safe and fun
c. Beneficial
d. Cheap
Answer a. Deceptive and designed to cheat people

Q9 The shopkeeper and his friends were
a. Working together to fool people
b. Friendly to Rasheed
c. Ignoring Rasheed
d. Honest
Answer a. Working together to fool people

Q10 Rasheed learns a valuable lesson about
a. Avoiding gambling and being cautious
b. Traveling to fairs
c. Avoiding his uncle
d. Playing only with friends
Answer a. Avoiding gambling and being cautious

Q11 The story "A Game of Chance" shows how some people
a. Use tricks to deceive others for money
b. Avoid crowds
c. Enjoy dancing
d. Study hard
Answer a. Use tricks to deceive others for money

Q12 Rasheed's uncle teaches him to
a. Be careful and avoid such games in the future
b. Spend all his money
c. Try again later
d. Avoid going to fairs
Answer a. Be careful and avoid such games in the future

Q13 Rasheed's reaction to losing all his money is
a. Disappointment and sadness
b. Excitement
c. Joy
d. Confusion
Answer a. Disappointment and sadness

Q14 The lesson Rasheed learns is to
a. Be cautious of games that promise easy rewards
b. Spend all his money
c. Ignore his uncle
d. Try gambling again
Answer a. Be cautious of games that promise easy rewards

Q15 The "lucky shop" in the story is actually a
a. Setup to trick people
b. Real store
c. Bakery
d. Workshop
Answer a. Setup to trick people

Q16 Rasheed's experience teaches readers about
a. The dangers of trusting strangers too quickly
b. The benefits of gambling
c. Trying games often
d. Keeping secrets
Answer a. The dangers of trusting strangers too quickly

Q17 Rasheed's uncle advised him because
a. He wanted to protect him from making bad choices
b. He was bored
c. He disliked games
d. He wanted Rasheed to play more
Answer a. He wanted to protect him from making bad choices

Q18 Rasheed learns that gambling can lead to
a. Loss and disappointment
b. Big rewards
c. Happiness
d. Great friendships
Answer a. Loss and disappointment

Q19 The shopkeeper's strategy is to
a. Make people think they can win easily
b. Give people free money
c. Keep everything quiet
d. Have no prizes
Answer a. Make people think they can win easily

Q20 The story "A Game of Chance" warns against
a. Being tempted by games of chance
b. Learning new games
c. Talking to strangers
d. Traveling alone
Answer a. Being tempted by games of chance

Chapter 15 - Vocation

Q1 The poem "Vocation" is about
a. A child's fascination with different professions
b. A trip to the city
c. A festival celebration
d. A family gathering
Answer a. A child's fascination with different professions

Q2 The child in the poem is curious about
a. Different jobs and what people do
b. Playing games
c. Cooking food
d. Traveling
Answer a. Different jobs and what people do

Q3 The child observes the bangle-seller on his way to
a. School
b. The market
c. The temple
d. The park
Answer a. School

Q4 The bangle-seller in the poem seems
a. Free to move around
b. Tired and sad
c. Very old
d. Angry
Answer a. Free to move around

Q5 The child admires the gardener because
a. He is free to dig the ground without anyone stopping him
b. He looks very strong
c. He has many plants
d. He is alone
Answer a. He is free to dig the ground without anyone stopping him

Q6 The child wants to be like the gardener so he can
a. Do things freely without restrictions
b. Sleep all day
c. Write books
d. Avoid work
Answer a. Do things freely without restrictions

Q7 The watchman's job is to
a. Stand guard at night
b. Sell fruits
c. Teach children
d. Drive a car
Answer a. Stand guard at night

Q8 The child is fascinated by the watchman because he
a. Walks alone at night and has freedom
b. Wears a uniform
c. Plays with children
d. Drives a car
Answer a. Walks alone at night and has freedom

Q9 In the poem, the child's wish reflects his
a. Desire to have freedom in life
b. Love for books
c. Passion for music
d. Interest in sports
Answer a. Desire to have freedom in life

Q10 The poem "Vocation" captures the child's view of
a. Different occupations and freedom
b. School rules
c. Family traditions
d. Science experiments
Answer a. Different occupations and freedom

Q11 The poem suggests that children often feel
a. Restricted by rules and long for freedom
b. Very independent
c. In control of everything
d. Uninterested in others' jobs
Answer a. Restricted by rules and long for freedom

Q12 The child in the poem thinks the bangle-seller has
a. A carefree life
b. Lots of money
c. Many friends
d. A difficult job
Answer a. A carefree life

Q13 The gardener's freedom to dig and play with soil makes the child
a. Wish for the same freedom in his life
b. Feel scared
c. Get tired
d. Ignore him
Answer a. Wish for the same freedom in his life

Q14 The child's admiration for the watchman shows his
a. Fascination with nighttime and solitude
b. Fear of darkness
c. Desire to avoid work
d. Love for uniforms
Answer a. Fascination with nighttime and solitude

Q15 The main theme of the poem is
a. A child's innocent longing for a life free from restrictions
b. Fear of the unknown
c. Love for animals
d. Importance of studying
Answer a. A child's innocent longing for a life free from restrictions

Q16 The poem "Vocation" highlights that children often see other jobs as
a. Free and exciting
b. Difficult
c. Boring
d. Scary
Answer a. Free and exciting

Q17 The child wishes to be the watchman because he
a. Wants to roam freely at night
b. Dislikes school
c. Loves uniforms
d. Wants to play games
Answer a. Wants to roam freely at night

Q18 In the poem, the child believes that adults have
a. More freedom and fewer restrictions
b. Difficult lives
c. No friends
d. A boring time
Answer a. More freedom and fewer restrictions

Q19 The poem portrays the child's desire to
a. Experience life without the limitations imposed by adults
b. Stay home
c. Avoid responsibilities
d. Stay with family
Answer a. Experience life without the limitations imposed by adults

Q20 The child's admiration for different jobs in the poem shows
a. His innocent view of freedom in adult life
b. His dislike for school
c. His anger towards others
d. His interest in studying
Answer a. His innocent view of freedom in adult life

Chapter 16 - Desert Animals

Q1 The chapter "Desert Animals" is about
a. How animals survive in desert conditions
b. Farm animals
c. Pets
d. Animals in the forest
Answer a. How animals survive in desert conditions

Q2 The desert environment is characterized by
a. Extreme heat and dryness
b. Heavy rainfall
c. Tall trees
d. Cold temperatures
Answer a. Extreme heat and dryness

Q3 Camels are often called
a. The "ships of the desert"
b. The "kings of the jungle"
c. The "fastest animals"
d. The "smallest animals"
Answer a. The "ships of the desert"

Q4 Camels can survive for days without
a. Water
b. Food
c. Rest
d. Walking
Answer a. Water

Q5 Rattlesnakes survive in the desert by
a. Hiding under rocks during the day
b. Flying
c. Running fast
d. Eating leaves
Answer a. Hiding under rocks during the day

Q6 Rattlesnakes are named for their
a. Rattling sound they make
b. Speed
c. Size
d. Color
Answer a. Rattling sound they make

Q7 Mongooses are known for their ability to
a. Fight snakes
b. Swim well
c. Fly
d. Dig deep holes
Answer a. Fight snakes

Q8 Desert foxes have large ears that help them
a. Cool down in the hot desert climate
b. Hear faraway sounds
c. Hide from enemies
d. Swim fast
Answer a. Cool down in the hot desert climate

Q9 Camels store fat in their
a. Humps
b. Stomachs
c. Legs
d. Heads
Answer a. Humps

Q10 The main theme of the chapter "Desert Animals" is
a. Adaptation and survival in extreme conditions
b. Speed and strength
c. Playing games
d. Living in the mountains
Answer a. Adaptation and survival in extreme conditions

Q11 Desert animals have adapted to their environment to
a. Survive harsh and extreme conditions
b. Live in water
c. Fly long distances
d. Avoid hunting
Answer a. Survive harsh and extreme conditions

Q12 How does the desert tortoise survive without water for long periods?
a. By storing water in its body
b. By eating plants
c. By hiding in holes
d. By sleeping during the day
Answer a. By storing water in its body

Q13 Many desert animals are nocturnal to
a. Avoid the daytime heat
b. Find food more easily
c. Enjoy the stars
d. Play with others
Answer a. Avoid the daytime heat

Q14 Mongooses are known for their
a. Ability to live in groups and fight off predators
b. Colorful feathers
c. Long legs
d. Loud voices
Answer a. Ability to live in groups and fight off predators

Q15 A common adaptation in desert animals is
a. Water conservation and efficient heat regulation
b. Thick fur
c. Bright colors
d. Large size
Answer a. Water conservation and efficient heat regulation

Q16 The desert environment supports life by
a. Allowing animals to adapt in unique ways
b. Providing plenty of water
c. Having tall trees
d. Staying cold
Answer a. Allowing animals to adapt in unique ways

Q17 Desert animals survive by
a. Adapting their behavior and bodies to the extreme climate
b. Living in water
c. Moving to cities
d. Staying with humans
Answer a. Adapting their behavior and bodies to the extreme climate

Q18 In the desert, animals like foxes have thick fur on their feet to
a. Protect them from the hot sand
b. Walk faster
c. Fly
d. Hide in the sand
Answer a. Protect them from the hot sand

Q19 The chapter teaches us that deserts are
a. Rich in life due to animals' unique adaptations
b. Empty and barren
c. Filled with only plants
d. Places with rain
Answer a. Rich in life due to animals' unique adaptations

Q20 The lesson from "Desert Animals" is that
a. Every environment has life adapted to survive in it
b. Deserts are dangerous places
c. Only reptiles live in deserts
d. Deserts have no plants
Answer a. Every environment has life adapted to survive in it

Chapter 17 - The Banyan Tree

Q1 The story "The Banyan Tree" is about
a. A boy's experience observing nature and wildlife
b. A trip to a museum
c. Building a treehouse
d. Meeting his friends
Answer a. A boy's experience observing nature and wildlife

Q2 The story is narrated by
a. A young boy
b. The boy's grandfather
c. A teacher
d. A gardener
Answer a. A young boy

Q3 The banyan tree in the story is described as
a. Very old and huge
b. Very small
c. Covered with flowers
d. Growing on a hill
Answer a. Very old and huge

Q4 Who is the boy's best friend in the story?
a. The banyan tree
b. His pet dog
c. His teacher
d. His classmate
Answer a. The banyan tree

Q5 The boy often sits on the tree's branches to
a. Watch birds, squirrels, and other creatures
b. Play with his friends
c. Write stories
d. Eat fruits
Answer a. Watch birds, squirrels, and other creatures

Q6 The boy shares the banyan tree with
a. Many animals and birds
b. Only his family
c. Only his friends
d. A group of neighbors
Answer a. Many animals and birds

Q7 The boy observes a memorable fight between
a. A mongoose and a cobra
b. Two squirrels
c. A parrot and a crow
d. A cat and a dog
Answer a. A mongoose and a cobra

Q8 The mongoose is described as being
a. Fearless and quick
b. Very slow
c. Very small
d. Brightly colored
Answer a. Fearless and quick

Q9 During the fight, the boy watches
a. From a safe spot on the tree
b. Very close to the fight
c. Through a fence
d. From a car
Answer a. From a safe spot on the tree

Q10 Who ultimately wins the fight between the mongoose and the cobra?
a. The mongoose
b. The cobra
c. The boy's pet dog
d. A hawk
Answer a. The mongoose

Q11 The boy feels a sense of adventure as he observes
a. The fierce battle and life in the banyan tree
b. His family working
c. His friends arriving
d. His garden blooming
Answer a. The fierce battle and life in the banyan tree

Q12 The story highlights the banyan tree as
a. A place of learning and wonder for the boy
b. A spot for gatherings
c. A hiding place
d. A school building
Answer a. A place of learning and wonder for the boy

Q13 The story "The Banyan Tree" emphasizes the theme of
a. The beauty and mystery of nature
b. Traveling far away
c. Building strong buildings
d. Avoiding animals
Answer a. The beauty and mystery of nature

Q14 The boy is fascinated by the mongoose's
a. Courage and agility in facing the cobra
b. Slow movements
c. Lack of interest in fighting
d. Fearful nature
Answer a. Courage and agility in facing the cobra

Q15 The banyan tree serves as
a. A sanctuary for both the boy and many creatures
b. A hiding spot for treasures
c. A dangerous place
d. A marketplace
Answer a. A sanctuary for both the boy and many creatures

Q16 The boy learns a lot by
a. Observing the interactions of animals in nature
b. Reading books
c. Going to the library
d. Playing video games
Answer a. Observing the interactions of animals in nature

Q17 The banyan tree in the story represents
a. Strength, life, and nature's wonders
b. Loneliness
c. Weakness
d. Fear
Answer a. Strength, life, and nature's wonders

Q18 The mongoose wins the fight by using its
a. Speed and clever tactics
b. Brute strength
c. Friends' help
d. Loud voice
Answer a. Speed and clever tactics

Q19 The story's setting on the banyan tree provides the boy with
a. A close connection to nature and wildlife
b. A study area
c. A place to store books
d. A hiding spot for games
Answer a. A close connection to nature and wildlife

Q20 The main lesson from "The Banyan Tree" is
a. Appreciating nature and its creatures
b. Avoiding animals
c. Becoming a hunter
d. Learning to fight
Answer a. Appreciating nature and its creatures

Chapter 18 - A Tale of Two Birds

Q1 The story "A Tale of Two Birds" is about
a. Two bird siblings who get separated
b. A farmer and his friend
c. A journey to the mountains
d. A festival celebration
Answer a. Two bird siblings who get separated

Q2 How do the two birds get separated?
a. A storm blows them away from each other
b. They are taken by a hunter
c. They decide to leave each other
d. A fire destroys their nest
Answer a. A storm blows them away from each other

Q3 One of the birds ends up living near
a. A cave with robbers
b. A beautiful garden
c. A lake
d. A palace
Answer a. A cave with robbers

Q4 The other bird lives near
a. A hermit's ashram
b. A mountain
c. A castle
d. A field
Answer a. A hermit's ashram

Q5 The bird that lives near the robbers becomes
a. Rough and aggressive
b. Quiet and shy
c. Very friendly
d. Frightened
Answer a. Rough and aggressive

Q6 The bird near the hermit's ashram learns to be
a. Polite and gentle
b. Aggressive
c. Fearful
d. Shy
Answer a. Polite and gentle

Q7 When the king hears the first bird speak, he is
a. Surprised and alarmed
b. Very happy
c. Amused
d. Annoyed
Answer a. Surprised and alarmed

Q8 The bird near the hermit's ashram welcomes the king
a. Politely and calmly
b. Loudly
c. By shouting
d. By ignoring him
Answer a. Politely and calmly

Q9 The king learns that the birds' behavior depends on
a. Their surroundings and company
b. Their age
c. The food they eat
d. Their feathers
Answer a. Their surroundings and company

Q10 The story teaches us the importance of
a. Good company and surroundings
b. Building nests
c. Traveling often
d. Finding treasures
Answer a. Good company and surroundings

Q11 The king is amazed to find that
a. The two birds, though similar, act differently
b. Birds can talk
c. Birds have different colors
d. Birds can fly high
Answer a. The two birds, though similar, act differently

Q12 The polite bird shows traits of
a. Kindness and gentleness
b. Aggression
c. Timidity
d. Fear
Answer a. Kindness and gentleness

Q13 The story "A Tale of Two Birds" demonstrates that behavior is influenced by
a. The people or environment around us
b. Only by family
c. The amount of food eaten
d. Traveling often
Answer a. The people or environment around us

Q14 The king's reaction to the birds' behavior is one of
a. Surprise and reflection
b. Anger
c. Sadness
d. Amusement
Answer a. Surprise and reflection

Q15 The robbers' bird reflects the traits of
a. Its surroundings and company
b. The forest
c. Its mother
d. The mountain
Answer a. Its surroundings and company

Q16 The story's lesson is about
a. How behavior and habits are influenced by those around us
b. Building a strong nest
c. Eating healthy food
d. Avoiding forests
Answer a. How behavior and habits are influenced by those around us

Q17 The hermit explains that the birds' behavior is due to
a. The company they keep
b. Their intelligence
c. Their diet
d. The time of day
Answer a. The company they keep

Q18 The king realizes that company can make someone
a. Kind or unkind depending on influence
b. Always smart
c. Very strong
d. Brave
Answer a. Kind or unkind depending on influence

Q19 The story suggests that to be good and wise, one should
a. Be in good company
b. Eat well
c. Travel often
d. Avoid others
Answer a. Be in good company

Q20 The polite bird learned its behavior from
a. The hermit and calm surroundings
b. The king
c. The robbers
d. Its family
Answer a. The hermit and calm surroundings

Chapter 19 - The Friendly Mongoose

Q1 The story "The Friendly Mongoose" is about
a. A family with a pet mongoose
b. A boy and his dog
c. A girl and her pet bird
d. A man and his horse
Answer a. A family with a pet mongoose

Q2 The mongoose was brought home to be a friend to
a. The family's baby
b. The father
c. The mother
d. The neighbor
Answer a. The family's baby

Q3 The mother was hesitant to leave the baby with the mongoose because
a. She was worried about the mongoose harming the baby
b. She didn't like animals
c. She thought it would run away
d. The baby was sleeping
Answer a. She was worried about the mongoose harming the baby

Q4 One day, the mother returned to find the mongoose with
a. Blood on its mouth and paws
b. A toy in its hand
c. Food for the baby
d. Another animal
Answer a. Blood on its mouth and paws

Q5 The mother assumed that the mongoose
a. Had attacked the baby
b. Was hurt
c. Was playing with the baby
d. Was cleaning itself
Answer a. Had attacked the baby

Q6 In her anger and fear, the mother
a. Killed the mongoose
b. Hugged the mongoose
c. Fed the mongoose
d. Ran away
Answer a. Killed the mongoose

Q7 After discovering her mistake, the mother realized that the mongoose had
a. Saved her baby from a snake
b. Hidden the baby
c. Left the house
d. Destroyed the toys
Answer a. Saved her baby from a snake

Q8 The story "The Friendly Mongoose" is a lesson about
a. Not jumping to conclusions
b. Being brave
c. Keeping pets
d. Traveling often
Answer a. Not jumping to conclusions

Q9 The snake in the story represents
a. Danger to the baby
b. A friend of the mongoose
c. A pet
d. A gift
Answer a. Danger to the baby

Q10 The mother's reaction was driven by
a. Fear and misunderstanding
b. Joy
c. Excitement
d. Curiosity
Answer a. Fear and misunderstanding

Q11 The mongoose is an example of
a. Loyalty and bravery
b. Fear and shyness
c. Speed and agility
d. Curiosity
Answer a. Loyalty and bravery

Q12 The mother's immediate action teaches us to
a. Think carefully before reacting
b. Avoid pets
c. Talk to others
d. Be quiet
Answer a. Think carefully before reacting

Q13 The family in the story lived
a. In a village
b. By the sea
c. In the mountains
d. Near a lake
Answer a. In a village

Q14 The story demonstrates that animals can be
a. Faithful and protective
b. Dangerous
c. Only wild
d. Ignorant
Answer a. Faithful and protective

Q15 The mother's misunderstanding led to
a. The tragic loss of a loyal pet
b. A lesson in patience
c. A new house
d. More pets
Answer a. The tragic loss of a loyal pet

Q16 The mongoose killed the snake to
a. Protect the baby
b. Play with it
c. Eat it
d. Get attention
Answer a. Protect the baby

Q17 The story teaches that assumptions can lead to
a. Regret and sadness
b. Excitement
c. Happiness
d. Laughter
Answer a. Regret and sadness

Q18 The mongoose displayed courage by
a. Fighting the snake to save the baby
b. Running away
c. Making noise
d. Hiding in a corner
Answer a. Fighting the snake to save the baby

Q19 The mother's regret is an example of
a. Guilt over an impulsive decision
b. Satisfaction
c. Excitement
d. Happiness
Answer a. Guilt over an impulsive decision

Q20 The story "The Friendly Mongoose" emphasizes the importance of
a. Patience and careful judgment
b. Traveling
c. Avoiding animals
d. Building strong houses
Answer a. Patience and careful judgment

Chapter 20 - The Shepherd's Treasure

Q1 "The Shepherd's Treasure" is about
a. An honest shepherd who is rewarded
b. A king and his soldiers
c. A festival in a village
d. A hunter and his dog
Answer a. An honest shepherd who is rewarded

Q2 The shepherd was known for his
a. Wisdom and kindness
b. Strength
c. Wealth
d. Anger
Answer a. Wisdom and kindness

Q3 The shepherd had no formal education but was
a. Wise and fair
b. Weak
c. Very rich
d. Always quiet
Answer a. Wise and fair

Q4 The king was impressed by the shepherd's
a. Honesty and intelligence
b. Clothes
c. Family
d. Jewelry
Answer a. Honesty and intelligence

Q5 The king made the shepherd the governor of a district because
a. He trusted his wisdom and honesty
b. He was his relative
c. He needed a friend
d. He wanted to avoid him
Answer a. He trusted his wisdom and honesty

Q6 The jealous courtiers accused the shepherd of
a. Stealing and hiding treasure
b. Being rude
c. Ignoring the king
d. Being lazy
Answer a. Stealing and hiding treasure

Q7 The shepherd kept a small, old chest as
a. A reminder of his humble origins
b. A treasure box
c. A weapon box
d. A food box
Answer a. A reminder of his humble origins

Q8 The chest contained
a. Only his old blanket
b. Gold coins
c. Weapons
d. Documents
Answer a. Only his old blanket

Q9 The shepherd's explanation of the chest showed his
a. Honesty and simplicity
b. Anger
c. Desire for wealth
d. Need for respect
Answer a. Honesty and simplicity

Q10 The story teaches that true wealth is in
a. Character and honesty, not material things
b. Collecting gold
c. Avoiding people
d. Wearing new clothes
Answer a. Character and honesty, not material things

Q11 The king's reaction to the shepherd's honesty was one of
a. Admiration and trust
b. Anger
c. Disappointment
d. Confusion
Answer a. Admiration and trust

Q12 The shepherd used the blanket as a symbol of
a. His humble beginnings
b. His new position
c. His wealth
d. His love for family
Answer a. His humble beginnings

Q13 The shepherd's simple life teaches us the importance of
a. Being humble and honest
b. Being very wealthy
c. Ignoring others
d. Avoiding hard work
Answer a. Being humble and honest

Q14 The jealous courtiers wanted to
a. Discredit the shepherd
b. Give him gifts
c. Invite him to dinner
d. Travel with him
Answer a. Discredit the shepherd

Q15 The shepherd became respected because he was
a. Wise, kind, and fair
b. Wealthy
c. Very famous
d. A warrior
Answer a. Wise, kind, and fair

Q16 The shepherd's old blanket symbolized
a. His humility and simple life
b. His love for gold
c. His wealth
d. His anger
Answer a. His humility and simple life

Q17 The courtiers' accusations were based on
a. Jealousy and suspicion
b. True events
c. The shepherd's wealth
d. Friendship
Answer a. Jealousy and suspicion

Q18 The shepherd's treasure was actually
a. His character and values
b. Gold coins
c. A large house
d. Expensive jewelry
Answer a. His character and values

Q19 The story's moral is that
a. True worth lies in a person's character, not in material possessions
b. Only the wealthy are respected
c. Fame is important
d. Avoiding others brings peace
Answer a. True worth lies in a person's character, not in material possessions

Q20 The king trusted the shepherd because he valued
a. Honesty and wisdom
b. Gold and silver
c. Expensive clothes
d. His palace
Answer a. Honesty and wisdom

Chapter 21 - Tansen

Q1 "Tansen" is about
a. A famous musician in Emperor Akbar's court
b. A king who built a palace
c. A soldier who fought many wars
d. A merchant who traveled far
Answer a. A famous musician in Emperor Akbar's court

Q2 Tansen is known for his skill in
a. Singing and playing musical instruments
b. Cooking
c. Dancing
d. Writing
Answer a. Singing and playing musical instruments

Q3 As a child, Tansen was fascinated by
a. The sounds of nature and music
b. Animals only
c. Traveling
d. Painting
Answer a. The sounds of nature and music

Q4 Tansen learned music from his guru
a. Swami Haridas
b. Akbar
c. Birbal
d. Mian Tansen
Answer a. Swami Haridas

Q5 Akbar's court was impressed with Tansen's
a. Musical talent
b. Wealth
c. Stories
d. Cooking skills
Answer a. Musical talent

Q6 Tansen's enemies wanted to test his skills by
a. Asking him to sing Raga Deepak
b. Giving him difficult tasks
c. Asking him to play games
d. Challenging him to a debate
Answer a. Asking him to sing Raga Deepak

Q7 Raga Deepak was known to
a. Generate intense heat
b. Bring rain
c. Calm the mind
d. Make people dance
Answer a. Generate intense heat

Q8 Tansen was afraid that singing Raga Deepak might
a. Burn him and everything around him
b. Make him lose his voice
c. Cause a flood
d. Make him invisible
Answer a. Burn him and everything around him

Q9 To counter the effects of Raga Deepak, Tansen asked
a. His daughter to sing Raga Megh
b. The emperor to protect him
c. His guru to help
d. His friends to sing along
Answer a. His daughter to sing Raga Megh

Q10 Raga Megh was expected to
a. Bring rain and cool the atmosphere
b. Make everyone sleepy
c. Make people laugh
d. Clear the skies
Answer a. Bring rain and cool the atmosphere

Q11 Tansen's singing of Raga Deepak created
a. Flames and intense heat
b. Snowfall
c. Silence
d. Strong winds
Answer a. Flames and intense heat

Q12 Tansen's daughter sang Raga Megh to
a. Save her father from the heat generated by Raga Deepak
b. Win the king's favor
c. Stop a war
d. Cure her father's illness
Answer a. Save her father from the heat generated by Raga Deepak

Q13 The story "Tansen" highlights the power of
a. Music and its effects on nature
b. Physical strength
c. Wealth
d. Fame
Answer a. Music and its effects on nature

Q14 Tansen became famous because of his
a. Unique ability to control nature through music
b. Kindness to animals
c. Travels to different places
d. Wealth and power
Answer a. Unique ability to control nature through music

Q15 Akbar admired Tansen for
a. His exceptional musical talent and dedication
b. His wealth
c. His family
d. His sense of humor
Answer a. His exceptional musical talent and dedication

Q16 Tansen's enemies hoped that Raga Deepak would
a. Harm him due to its intense heat
b. Bring him wealth
c. Make him famous
d. Stop him from singing
Answer a. Harm him due to its intense heat

Q17 Tansen is remembered as one of the
a. Greatest musicians in Indian history
b. Wealthiest men
c. Best kings
d. Most powerful generals
Answer a. Greatest musicians in Indian history

Q18 The story of Tansen teaches that true talent
a. Can overcome all challenges
b. Requires wealth
c. Comes from fear
d. Is only inherited
Answer a. Can overcome all challenges

Q19 The main lesson from "Tansen" is about
a. The power of dedication and talent
b. The importance of wealth
c. Ignoring talents
d. Avoiding music
Answer a. The power of dedication and talent

Q20 Tansen's story is an inspiration for those who
a. Aspire to pursue their passion
b. Want to travel
c. Seek fame only
d. Avoid hard work
Answer a. Aspire to pursue their passion

Chapter 22 - The Monkey and the Crocodile

Q1 The story "The Monkey and the Crocodile" is about
a. Friendship and betrayal between a monkey and a crocodile
b. A monkey's family
c. A crocodile's journey
d. A group of animals in the jungle
Answer a. Friendship and betrayal between a monkey and a crocodile

Q2 The monkey lived
a. On a tree near the river
b. In a village
c. Near the ocean
d. On a hill
Answer a. On a tree near the river

Q3 The monkey and the crocodile became friends because
a. The monkey shared fruits with the crocodile
b. They grew up together
c. They both liked to swim
d. The monkey helped the crocodile find food
Answer a. The monkey shared fruits with the crocodile

Q4 The crocodile's wife wanted to eat
a. The monkey's heart
b. Fruits from the tree
c. Fish
d. Grass
Answer a. The monkey's heart

Q5 The crocodile felt torn between
a. His friendship with the monkey and his wife's wishes
b. His love for food and his family
c. Staying home and swimming
d. His friends and his children
Answer a. His friendship with the monkey and his wife's wishes

Q6 The crocodile finally agreed to
a. Take the monkey to his wife
b. Avoid the monkey
c. Share fruits with the monkey
d. Swim alone
Answer a. Take the monkey to his wife

Q7 When the monkey realized the crocodile's intentions, he
a. Thought of a clever plan to escape
b. Fought the crocodile
c. Called for help
d. Ignored it
Answer a. Thought of a clever plan to escape

Q8 The monkey told the crocodile he had left his heart
a. On the tree
b. In the water
c. At the riverbank
d. With his family
Answer a. On the tree

Q9 The crocodile took the monkey back to the tree because he
a. Believed the monkey's story
b. Wanted to live in the tree
c. Wanted to bring more fruits
d. Felt sleepy
Answer a. Believed the monkey's story

Q10 The monkey managed to escape by
a. Climbing back onto the tree
b. Jumping into the water
c. Fighting the crocodile
d. Running away
Answer a. Climbing back onto the tree

Q11 The story teaches a lesson about
a. Intelligence and quick thinking
b. Building a house
c. Swimming well
d. Working together
Answer a. Intelligence and quick thinking

Q12 The crocodile's wife represents
a. Greed and betrayal
b. Kindness
c. Honesty
d. Humor
Answer a. Greed and betrayal

Q13 The monkey's clever escape highlights his
a. Wit and intelligence
b. Strength
c. Fear
d. Sadness
Answer a. Wit and intelligence

Q14 The monkey learned not to trust the crocodile again because
a. He had tried to deceive him
b. He ate all the fruits
c. He disliked water
d. He had other friends
Answer a. He had tried to deceive him

Q15 The story "The Monkey and the Crocodile" teaches us about
a. Trusting our instincts and being cautious in friendships
b. Growing trees
c. Swimming often
d. Traveling alone
Answer a. Trusting our instincts and being cautious in friendships

Q16 The moral of the story is that one should
a. Be careful in trusting others
b. Always help friends
c. Avoid making new friends
d. Live alone
Answer a. Be careful in trusting others

Q17 The monkey's clever thinking saved him from
a. Being eaten by the crocodile
b. Falling into the water
c. Getting lost
d. Losing his home
Answer a. Being eaten by the crocodile

Q18 The crocodile's plan backfires when he
a. Realizes he has been tricked by the monkey
b. Leaves the monkey alone
c. Attacks other animals
d. Fails to catch fish
Answer a. Realizes he has been tricked by the monkey

Q19 The story shows that animals can also have
a. Cleverness similar to humans
b. Weaknesses
c. Fear
d. Loneliness
Answer a. Cleverness similar to humans

Q20 The monkey's final words to the crocodile suggest that
a. Intelligence can defeat strength
b. Friendship is important
c. Animals should never fight
d. Food is essential
Answer a. Intelligence can defeat strength

Chapter 23 - The Wonder Called Sleep

Q1 "The Wonder Called Sleep" explains the importance of
a. Sleep for health and well-being
b. Eating
c. Studying
d. Exercising
Answer a. Sleep for health and well-being

Q2 The chapter describes sleep as
a. A natural and essential process
b. A waste of time
c. Unnecessary for children
d. Only for the elderly
Answer a. A natural and essential process

Q3 Sleep helps in
a. Restoring energy and repairing the body
b. Increasing hunger
c. Making one lazy
d. Reducing intelligence
Answer a. Restoring energy and repairing the body

Q4 According to the chapter, during sleep, the body
a. Performs important functions without our awareness
b. Stops all functions
c. Only digests food
d. Does nothing
Answer a. Performs important functions without our awareness

Q5 The author mentions that lack of sleep can lead to
a. Health issues and decreased productivity
b. More energy
c. Happiness
d. Less need for food
Answer a. Health issues and decreased productivity

Q6 Different animals have varying sleep patterns based on
a. Their natural instincts and environments
b. Their age
c. Their size
d. Their diet
Answer a. Their natural instincts and environments

Q7 The chapter highlights that sleep is also essential for
a. Learning and memory retention
b. Forgetting things
c. Avoiding responsibilities
d. Daydreaming
Answer a. Learning and memory retention

Q8 The author mentions that newborns need more sleep than
a. Adults
b. Teenagers
c. Elderly people
d. Children
Answer a. Adults

Q9 During deep sleep, the body is said to be
a. At its most restful state
b. Active and alert
c. Unconscious
d. Always dreaming
Answer a. At its most restful state

Q10 Sleep is often described as a
a. Time for the mind and body to rejuvenate
b. Boring activity
c. Time wasted
d. Unnecessary chore
Answer a. Time for the mind and body to rejuvenate

Q11 People who do not get enough sleep may experience
a. Irritability and reduced concentration
b. Increased productivity
c. Better mood
d. Improved health
Answer a. Irritability and reduced concentration

Q12 The chapter suggests that establishing a sleep routine can help
a. Improve sleep quality and duration
b. Increase wakefulness
c. Make one feel restless
d. Create confusion
Answer a. Improve sleep quality and duration

Q13 The chapter implies that sleep affects
a. Both physical and mental health
b. Only physical health
c. Only mental health
d. Social skills
Answer a. Both physical and mental health

Q14 The author encourages readers to view sleep as
a. A necessary and valuable part of life
b. A luxury
c. A sign of laziness
d. A burden
Answer a. A necessary and valuable part of life

Q15 The chapter mentions that many cultures have unique
a. Sleep traditions and rituals
b. Sleeping pills
c. Nighttime parties
d. Work schedules
Answer a. Sleep traditions and rituals

Q16 The author encourages young people to prioritize
a. Healthy sleep habits
b. Staying up late
c. Watching TV
d. Playing games
Answer a. Healthy sleep habits

Q17 The benefits of sleep include
a. Enhanced creativity and problem-solving skills
b. Less energy
c. More anxiety
d. Forgetting things
Answer a. Enhanced creativity and problem-solving skills

Q18 The chapter "The Wonder Called Sleep" encourages readers to
a. Appreciate the importance of sleep
b. Ignore sleep
c. Stay awake longer
d. Sleep less
Answer a. Appreciate the importance of sleep

Q19 Overall, the chapter emphasizes that
a. Sleep is essential for overall health and wellness
b. Sleep should be avoided
c. Sleep is only for children
d. Sleep has no benefits
Answer a. Sleep is essential for overall health and wellness

Q20 The conclusion of the chapter reminds us that
a. Quality sleep is a key to a happy and healthy life
b. Working late is better
c. Staying awake is important
d. Napping is for lazy people
Answer a. Quality sleep is a key to a happy and healthy life

Chapter 24 - A Pact with the Sun

Q1 "A Pact with the Sun" tells the story of
a. A young girl and her struggles with the sun
b. A boy and his dream to travel
c. A king and his subjects
d. A man and his journey to the stars
Answer a. A young girl and her struggles with the sun

Q2 The story begins with the introduction of
a. A girl named Saeeda and her sick mother
b. A boy named Ravi and his adventure
c. A wise old man
d. A village festival
Answer a. A girl named Saeeda and her sick mother

Q3 Saeeda's mother is suffering from
a. An illness that requires sunlight for healing
b. A cold
c. Fatigue
d. A broken leg
Answer a. An illness that requires sunlight for healing

Q4 The doctor advises Saeeda's mother to
a. Get plenty of sunshine
b. Stay indoors
c. Eat more food
d. Sleep less
Answer a. Get plenty of sunshine

Q5 Saeeda makes a pact with the sun to
a. Shine bright and help her mother heal
b. Stay hidden
c. Go away
d. Never shine again
Answer a. Shine bright and help her mother heal

Q6 The sun responds to Saeeda's request by
a. Shining brightly and spreading warmth
b. Hiding behind clouds
c. Ignoring her completely
d. Becoming angry
Answer a. Shining brightly and spreading warmth

Q7 The mother starts to feel better when
a. The sun shines directly on her
b. She drinks warm soup
c. Saeeda sings to her
d. She sleeps more
Answer a. The sun shines directly on her

Q8 The story emphasizes the role of
a. Nature in healing and well-being
b. Medicines only
c. Traveling
d. Avoiding sunlight
Answer a. Nature in healing and well-being

Q9 Saeeda's determination to help her mother shows her
a. Love and care for her family
b. Fear of the sun
c. Desire to play
d. Interest in gardening
Answer a. Love and care for her family

Q10 The sun is depicted as a
a. Caring and nurturing force in the story
b. Cold and distant
c. Angry at people
d. Only for the rich
Answer a. Caring and nurturing force in the story

Q11 The mother's improvement signifies
a. The healing power of sunlight
b. The importance of food
c. The need for medicine
d. The effectiveness of rest
Answer a. The healing power of sunlight

Q12 The chapter concludes with the idea that
a. Nature plays a vital role in our health
b. Animals should be kept safe
c. Music heals
d. Sleep is the only cure
Answer a. Nature plays a vital role in our health

Q13 The story encourages readers to appreciate
a. The sun and its effects on life
b. The moon's beauty
c. Rainy days
d. Cold weather
Answer a. The sun and its effects on life

Q14 Saeeda's belief in the sun reflects a
a. Hopeful and positive outlook
b. Fearful attitude
c. Negative perspective
d. Distrust in nature
Answer a. Hopeful and positive outlook

Q15 The chapter ultimately conveys that
a. We should respect and care for nature
b. We should avoid going outdoors
c. We need to ignore the sun
d. Nature is only for enjoyment
Answer a. We should respect and care for nature

Q16 Saeeda's actions demonstrate the power of
a. Faith and determination in difficult times
b. Anger and frustration
c. Fear of losing
d. Disinterest in health
Answer a. Faith and determination in difficult times

Q17 The sun's rays symbolize
a. Hope, life, and healing
b. Fear
c. Weakness
d. Trouble
Answer a. Hope, life, and healing

Q18 The relationship between Saeeda and the sun can be seen as a
a. Pact of trust and mutual respect
b. One-sided expectation
c. Confusion
d. Disagreement
Answer a. Pact of trust and mutual respect

Q19 The story concludes with a reminder that
a. Nature's elements can greatly influence our lives
b. We should avoid nature
c. Technology is better than nature
d. Sunlight is harmful
Answer a. Nature's elements can greatly influence our lives

Q20 The overall message of "A Pact with the Sun" is that
a. Nature provides essential support for our well-being
b. We should not rely on nature
c. Animals are more important than plants
d. Only humans can help each other
Answer a. Nature provides essential support for our well-being

English Grammar

Q1 A noun is a word that represents a
a. Person, place, or thing
b. Action
c. Description
d. Emotion
Answer a. Person, place, or thing

Q2 Which of the following is a collective noun?
a. Team
b. Book
c. Happiness
d. Run
Answer a. Team

Q3 Which of the following is a proper noun?
a. city
b. London
c. river
d. animal
Answer b. London

Q4 What type of noun is 'friendship'?
a. Abstract noun
b. Collective noun
c. Proper noun
d. Concrete noun
Answer a. Abstract noun

Q5 Choose the plural form of 'child'.
a. Childs
b. Children
c. Childes
d. Childer
Answer b. Children

Q6 Identify the common noun in the sentence: "The cat chased the mouse."
a. Cat
b. Chased
c. Mouse
d. The
Answer a. Cat

Q7 Which sentence contains a countable noun?
a. Water is essential for life.
b. I have three apples.
c. Love is powerful.
d. Happiness is fleeting.
Answer b. I have three apples.

Q8 The word 'information' is a
a. Countable noun
b. Uncountable noun
c. Proper noun
d. Collective noun
Answer b. Uncountable noun

Q9 Which of the following is an example of a compound noun?
a. Toothpaste
b. Water
c. Happiness
d. School
Answer a. Toothpaste

Q10 Choose the sentence with the correct noun usage.
a. The sheeps are grazing in the field.
b. The sheep are grazing in the field.
c. The sheeps is grazing in the field.
d. The sheepses are grazing in the field.
Answer b. The sheep are grazing in the field.

Q11 A pronoun is used to
a. Replace a noun
b. Describe a verb
c. Connect sentences
d. Show emotion
Answer a. Replace a noun

Q12 Which of the following is a personal pronoun?
a. He
b. All
c. Many
d. Group
Answer a. He

Q13 Choose the correct pronoun for the sentence: "This is my brother; _____ is very tall."
a. He
b. She
c. They
d. It
Answer a. He

Q14 Which pronoun would replace 'the teacher' in the sentence: "The teacher gave us homework"?
a. She
b. They
c. He
d. All of the above
Answer d. All of the above

Q15 Identify the reflexive pronoun in the sentence: "She made herself a sandwich."
a. Made
b. Herself
c. Sandwich
d. She
Answer b. Herself

Q16 The word 'them' is an example of a
a. Demonstrative pronoun
b. Indefinite pronoun
c. Personal pronoun
d. Interrogative pronoun
Answer c. Personal pronoun

Q17 Which of the following sentences contains a relative pronoun?
a. The girl who won the race is my friend.
b. He is a good player.
c. I like pizza.
d. She sings beautifully.
Answer a. The girl who won the race is my friend.

Q18 Choose the correct possessive pronoun: "That book is _____."
a. Mine
b. My
c. I
d. Me
Answer a. Mine

Q19 Which pronoun is used to ask questions?
a. Interrogative pronoun
b. Demonstrative pronoun
c. Indefinite pronoun
d. Personal pronoun
Answer a. Interrogative pronoun

Q20 The word 'anyone' is an example of a
a. Personal pronoun
b. Reflexive pronoun
c. Indefinite pronoun
d. Possessive pronoun
Answer c. Indefinite pronoun

Q21 A verb is a word that expresses
a. Action or state of being
b. Nouns
c. Descriptions
d. Connections
Answer a. Action or state of being

Q22 Which of the following is an action verb?
a. Run
b. Beautiful
c. Quickly
d. Happiness
Answer a. Run

Q23 In the sentence "She dances gracefully," the verb is
a. Dances
b. She
c. Gracefully
d. None
Answer a. Dances

Q24 The verb 'to be' can be used as
a. An action verb only
b. A linking verb
c. Only a helping verb
d. A regular verb
Answer b. A linking verb

Q25 Identify the auxiliary verb in the sentence: "She is reading a book."
a. Is
b. Reading
c. She
d. Book
Answer a. Is

Q26 Which sentence contains a transitive verb?
a. She kicked the ball.
b. He sleeps.
c. They run every day.
d. She is happy.
Answer a. She kicked the ball.

Q27 The main verb in the sentence "They are playing football" is
a. Are
b. Playing
c. They
d. Football
Answer b. Playing

Q28 Which of the following is a linking verb?
a. Jump
b. Is
c. Run
d. Write
Answer b. Is

Q29 The verb tense describes
a. When the action occurs
b. The type of noun
c. The subject of the sentence
d. The mood of the speaker
Answer a. When the action occurs

Q30 Which of the following sentences is in the past tense?
a. I will go to the store.
b. I am going to the store.
c. I went to the store.
d. I go to the store.
Answer c. I went to the store.

Q31 Tenses are used to indicate
a. The time of an action
b. The type of sentence
c. The length of sentences
d. The importance of subjects
Answer a. The time of action

Q32 Which form of the verb is correct in the present continuous tense?
a. He is playing.
b. He plays.
c. He played.
d. He will play.
Answer a. He is playing.

Q33 Identify the future tense in the following sentences:
a. She will dance at the party.
b. She dances at the party.
c. She danced at the party.
d. She is dancing at the party.
Answer a. She will dance at the party.

Q34 The past perfect tense is used to describe
a. An action that was completed before another action in the past
b. An ongoing action in the past
c. A future action
d. A current action
Answer a. An action that was completed before another action in the past

Q35 Which sentence uses the correct tense?
a. I will eat dinner at 7 PM.
b. I am eating dinner at 7 PM.
c. I eat dinner at 7 PM.
d. I eat dinner at 7 PM.
Answer a. I will eat dinner at 7 PM.

Q36 The structure of the simple present tense is typically
a. Subject + base form of the verb
b. Subject + was/were + verb
c. Subject + will + verb
d. Subject + is/am/are + verb
Answer a. Subject + base form of the verb

Q37 Identify the correct sentence in the past tense.
a. They went to school yesterday.
b. They went to school yesterday.
c. They went to school yesterday.
d. They went to school yesterday.
Answer c. They went to school yesterday.

Q38 The present perfect tense is formed using
a. Have/has + past participle
b. Was/were + verb
c. Is/am/are + verb
d. Will + base form
Answer a. Have/has + past participle.

Q39 Choose the correct sentence in future tense.
a. She plays the guitar tomorrow.
b. She will play the guitar tomorrow.
c. She will play the guitar tomorrow.
d. She is playing the guitar tomorrow.
Answer b. She will play the guitar tomorrow.

Q40 Which sentence is in passive voice?
a. John threw the ball.
b. John throws the ball.
c. John is throwing the ball.
d. John will throw the ball.
Answer: a. John threw the ball.

Q41 Identify the active voice sentence.
a. The children ate the cake.
b. The children ate the cake.
c. The cake is being eaten.
d. The cake has been eaten.
Answer b. The children ate the cake.

Q42 The passive voice is used when
a. The focus is on the action or the receiver of the action
b. The subject performs the action
c. The action is not important
d. The subject is always active
Answer a. The focus is on the action or the receiver of the action

Q43 In the sentence "Mary read the book," the subject is
a. The book
b. Was read
c. Mary
d. By
Answer a. The book

Q44 Which of the following is an adjective?
a. Run
b. Beautiful
c. Quickly
d. Eat
Answer b. Beautiful

Q45 Adjectives are used to describe
a. Nouns
b. Verbs
c. Pronouns
d. Adverbs
Answer a. Nouns

Q46 Choose the sentence that uses an adjective correctly.
a. She runs fast.
b. The cake is delicious.
c. He sings well.
d. They are happily dancing.
Answer b. The cake is delicious.

Q47 Which of the following sentences contains a comparative adjective?
a. She is the most brilliant student.
b. He is taller than his brother.
c. This is a beautiful flower.
d. The soup is hot.
Answer b. He is taller than his brother.

Q48 Identify the excellent form in this sentence: "She is the fastest runner."
a. Fast
b. Faster
c. Fastest
d. Running
Answer c. Fastest

Q49 What is the adjective in the sentence: "The tall building is new"?
a. Tall
b. Building
c. New
d. Is
Answer a. Tall

Q50 The adjective "red" in the sentence "I have a red car" describes
a. The color of the car
b. The size of the car
c. The model of the car
d. The type of car
Answer a. The colour of the car

Q51 An adverb modifies
a. A noun
b. A verb, adjective, or another adverb
c. A pronoun
d. A conjunction
Answer b. A verb, adjective, or another adverb

Q52 Which of the following is an adverb?
a. Quickly
b. Happy
c. Book
d. Blue
Answer a. Quickly

Q53 In the sentence "She sings beautifully," the adverb describes
a. The subject
b. The verb
c. The object
d. The adjective
Answer b. The verb

Q54 Which sentence uses an adverb correctly?
a. He dashed to the store.
b. She danced gracefully.
c. They finished the work quickly.
d. The cat jumped highly.
Answer c. They finished the work quickly.

Q55 Identify the adverb in the sentence: "He spoke very softly."
a. Spoke
b. Very
c. Softly
d. He
Answer c. Softly

Q56 Which of the following sentences uses a comparative adverb?
a. She runs faster than her brother.
b. He sings well.
c. They finished the project quickly.
d. The dog barked loudly.
Answer a. She runs faster than her brother.

Q57 An example of a conjunction is
a. And
b. Quickly
c. Red
d. Cat
Answer a. And

Q58 Conjunctions are used to
a. Connect words, phrases, or clauses
b. Describe nouns
c. Show action
d. Make sentences longer
Answer a. Connect words, phrases, or clauses

Q59 Which sentence contains a coordinating conjunction?
a. I want to go to the party, but I am busy.
b. The cat ran away.
c. She is happy.
d. They are playing.
Answer a. I want to attend the party but am busy.

Q60 Identify the subordinating conjunction in the sentence: "Although it was raining, we went for a walk."
a. Although
b. It
c. Was
d. Went
Answer a. Although

Q61 Which of the following is an example of a compound sentence?
a. I like ice cream, and I also like cake.
b. I like ice cream.
c. Ice cream is delicious.
d. I run every morning.
Answer a. I like ice cream, and I also like cake.

Q62 The purpose of a preposition is to
a. Show the relationship between a noun or pronoun and other words in a sentence
b. Replace a noun
c. Connect ideas
d. State an action
Answer a. Show the relationship between a noun or pronoun and other words in a sentence.

Q63 Which of the following is a preposition?
a. Quickly
b. Under
c. Beautiful
d. Jump
Answer b. Under

Q64 Choose the correct preposition to complete the sentence: "The cat is hiding _____ on the table."
a. Under
b. Over
c. Between
d. Near
Answer a. Under

Q65 In the sentence "She sat on the chair," the preposition is
a. Sat
b. On
c. The
d. Chair
Answer b. On

Q66 Which sentence uses the preposition correctly?
a. The dog is running in the park.
b. She is walking to the shop.
c. They are swimming at the pool.
d. All of the above.
Answer d. All of the above.

Q67 A conjunction connects
a. Words, phrases, or clauses
b. Subjects and verbs
c. Adjectives and nouns
d. Sentences only
Answer a. Words, phrases, or clauses.

Q68 Which of the following sentences contains a correlative conjunction?
a. Neither the dog nor the cat is here.
b. I want to go, but I am tired.
c. She is happy and cheerful.
d. He eats pizza and pasta.
Answer a. Neither the dog nor the cat is here.

Q69 Which of the following is not a punctuation mark?
a. Period
b. Comma
c. Verb
d. Question mark
Answer c. Verb

Q70 A period is used to
a. End a declarative sentence
b. Show Excitement
c. Indicate a pause
d. Ask a question
Answer a. End a declarative sentence.

Q71 Which sentence requires a question mark?
a. I love to read books.
b. What time is it
c. She enjoys swimming.
d. They are going to the park.
Answer b. What time is it

Q72 A comma is used to
a. Separate items in a list
b. End a sentence
c. Indicate a pause between ideas
d. All of the above
Answer d. All of the above

Q73 In the sentence "Let's eat, Grandma," the comma is necessary to
a. Separate the two actions
b. Clarify who is being addressed
c. Indicate a pause
d. Show Excitement
Answer b. Clarify who is being addressed

Q74 A quotation mark is used to
a. Enclose direct speech
b. End a sentence
c. Indicate a pause
d. Show possession
Answer a. Enclose direct speech.

Q75 Identify the correct use of an apostrophe.
a. The dog wagged its tail.
b. The dog wagged its tail.
c. The dogs wagged their tails.
d. The dog wagged their tail.
Answer a. The dog wagged its tail.

Q76 Which of the following sentences uses punctuation correctly?
a. I went to the store and bought apples, oranges, and bananas.
b. She said, "Hello!"
c. Can you come over here
d. The book is on the table; it is red
Answer b. She said, "Hello!"

Q77 A semicolon is used to
a. Join two related independent clauses
b. End a sentence
c. Separate items in a list
d. Indicate a pause
Answer a. Join two related independent clauses

Q78 In the sentence "He is going to the store," the word "to" is a
a. Verb
b. Preposition
c. Conjunction
d. Adverb
Answer b. Preposition

Q79 A declarative sentence makes a
a. Statement
b. Question
c. Command
d. Exclamation
Answer a. Statement

Q80 The function of an exclamation mark is to
a. Show excitement or strong emotion
b. End a question
c. Make a statement
d. Separate items
Answer a. Show excitement or strong emotion

Q81 Identify the error in the sentence: "She doesn't like apples."
a. Dont should be, doesn't
b. Like should be liked
c. Apples should be apple
d. She is correct
Answer a. Dont should be, doesn't

Q82 Choose the correct sentence:
a. It's raining outside.
b. It's raining outside.
c. It's raining outside.
d. It is raining outside.
Answer b. It's raining outside.

Q83 The phrase "running fast" in "She was running fast" describes
a. The subject
b. The verb
c. The object
d. The conjunction
Answer b. The verb

Q84 A subject in a sentence typically indicates
a. Who or what the sentence is about
b. The action of the sentence
c. The object of the sentence
d. The adjective
Answer a. Who or what the sentence is about

Q85 A complete sentence must have at least
a. A subject and a verb
b. An adjective
c. An adverb
d. A preposition
Answer a. A subject and a verb

Q86 The sentence "She runs every morning" is an example of a
a. Simple sentence
b. Compound sentence
c. Complex sentence
d. Interrogative sentence
Answer a. Simple sentence.

Q87 Which sentence is compound?
a. I wanted to walk, but it started to rain.
b. She enjoys reading.
c. He runs every day.
d. The cat sleeps on the mat.
Answer a. I wanted to walk, but it started to rain.

Q88 The term "subject-verb agreement" refers to
a. The subject and verb must match in number
b. The subject must be longer than the verb
c. The verb must be in past tense
d. The subject must be a noun
Answer a. The subject and verb must match in number

Q89 In the sentence "The dogs bark loudly," the subject is
a. Dogs
b. Bark
c. Loudly
d. The
Answer a. Dogs

Q90 In reported speech, the verb "said" is typically followed by
a. A question
b. A statement
c. An object
d. A quote
Answer b. A statement

Q91 Which of the following is an example of indirect speech?
a. She said, "I am happy."
b. She said that she was happy.
c. She said, "I was happy."
d. She says that she is happy.
Answer b. She said that she was happy.

Q92 Which of the following is the correct way to frame a question?
a. What is your name?
b. Your name is what?
c. What is your name?
d. Is your name what?
Answer a. What is your name?

Q93 Choose the correct form of the sentence: "She _____ to the party last night."
a. Go
b. Goes
c. Went
d. Going
Answer c. Went

Q94 The correct sentence is:
a. Everyone was happy.
b. Everyone was happy.
c. Everyone is happy.
d. Everyone is happy.
Answer b. Everyone was happy.

Q95 A notice typically includes
a. The date and purpose of the announcement
b. A long explanation
c. Personal opinions
d. Complex language
Answer a. The date and purpose of the announcement

Q96 Which of the following is a feature of a formal letter?
a. Casual language
b. No subject line
c. Proper salutation and closing
d. Use of contractions
Answer c. Proper salutation and closing

Q97 A diary entry is often written in
a. Informal language
b. Complex sentences
c. Passive voice
d. Formal tone
Answer a. Informal language.

Q98 In a debate, participants typically
a. Argue both sides of an issue
b. Speak without preparation
c. Only express personal opinions
d. Avoid conflict
Answer a. Argue both sides of an issue

Q99 An article should have
a. A clear introduction, body, and conclusion
b. Long paragraphs
c. No headings
d. Complex vocabulary only
Answer a. A clear introduction, body, and conclusion

Q100 A speech is often intended to
a. Inform, persuade, or entertain an audience
b. Confuse listeners
c. Avoid communication
d. Only express personal feelings
Answer a. Inform, persuade, or entertain an audience.